APPLIED MEASUREMENT IN EDUCATION, *19*(3), 185–187
Copyright © 2006, Lawrence Erlbaum Associates, Inc.

T0316021

GUEST EDITOR'S INTRODUCTION

An Introduction to Multistage Testing

Alan D. Mead

PAQ Services, Inc.
Bellingham, Washington

This issue of *Applied Measurement in Education* contains a series of articles examining aspects of multistage testing (MST), also called computerized adaptive sequential testing (CAST). MST is a test administration method whereby examinees are routed to later tests on the basis of their performances on routing tests. Examinees who fare poorly on routing tests complete easier levels in subsequent stages. Thus, multistage tests are adaptive but otherwise have important differences as compared to computerized adaptive tests.

EVOLUTION OF MULTISTAGE TESTING

MST is not a new idea. A kind of noncomputerized MST was developed prior to computerized adaptive tests (CAT; Lord, 1971, 1980, chap. 9). However, MST research was eclipsed by CAT: Creative use of item response theory and computers raised the potential to create tests that were shorter than their predecessors and yet had greater reliability. Today, different varieties of item-level adaptive tests enjoy widespread use, and CAT has fulfilled its potential to make assessment more efficient. Nonetheless, as CATs began to be used in practice, certain practical shortcomings became evident, and a modern variety of MST arose to address these issues.

The first practical issue is that item-level adaptive tests require a kind of "on-the-fly" automated test assembly (ATA) that must occur in the field at the time of testing. This sometimes meant that the ATA was more limited than might be the

Correspondence should be addressed to Alan D. Mead, PAQ Services, Inc., 1226 Keywest Drive, Lockport, IL 60441. E-mail: amead@alanmead.org

Psychology Press
Taylor & Francis Group

New York London

case if the test were assembled "in house." For example, complex content specifications might need to be relaxed for CAT. Or the CAT might sometimes miss the specifications because its sequential ATA was not always optimal. Also, software bugs or design flaws could cause unintended test assembly. In addition, some exams have content requirements that are difficult to quantify or implement as rules. Subject matter experts and other stakeholders sometimes feel disenfranchised because the tests are literally assembled in the field, without their direct influence or review. MST solves this problem by moving ATA in house and allowing for subject matter expert input and review prior to publication.

As they are commonly implemented, CAT administration forces examinees to abandon some of their favorite test-taking strategies. For example, it is common to prohibit item review and skipping for fear that examinees will use these features to circumvent the adaptive algorithm and thus the exam. Because MST stages are static, examinees may be allowed unfettered skip-and-review within a stage without concern for the integrity of the exam.

Finally, the nature of individualized test forms directly implies that the resulting item response matrix will be sparse, with the few nonmissing values scattered across the data record. This sparse matrix of item response vectors precludes many traditional statistical techniques. For example, it is difficult to conduct differential item functioning analyses or rescale items using such sparse data. The sparse data arising from MST are block sparse and more tractable to statistical analysis.

Thus, these practical problems are ameliorated or completely solved by MST. In addition, because the test forms are designed before they are deployed, additional security can be built into the exam. For example, MST test developers should never get back results and find that 20% of the items in the pool are used on 80% of examinees' tests (as is common in CAT settings; Wainer, 2000). In evolutionary terms, MST is a new kind of test administration closely related to CAT but having evolved certain features that may make it a better fit to the environment of some examination programs.

THIS SPECIAL ISSUE

As a set, these four articles and the commentary provide a comprehensive introduction to the state of the practice of multistage testing. The first article, by Luecht, Brumfield, and Breithaupt (2006/this issue), describes MST, addresses some common practical considerations for MSTs, and then discusses a key technology: ATA.

The next two articles examine likely MST configurations and demonstrate the conditions under which MSTs are psychometrically compelling. Jodoin, Zenisky, and Hambleton's (2006/this issue) study compares different MST designs. In the context of a highly reliable test, they show that MSTs have measurement accuracy comparable to nonadaptive fixed-length tests and that two different MST designs produced similar results. This study also illustrates the strong influences of the item pool and ATA on MST performance. Hambleton and Xing's (2006/this issue) article extends these findings by examining additional designs, comparing MSTs to linear forms and item-level adaptive exams, and examining different item pool conditions. They found that MSTs solve practical problems but still perform psychometrically like linear forms and nearly as well as item-level adaptive tests.

The article by Chuah, Drasgow, and Luecht (2006/this issue) examines the sample sizes needed for MSTs. Smaller samples allow testing agencies to produce larger, more secure item pools. The authors explore the effects of different item calibration sample sizes on latent person ability estimation and licensure classification accuracy. Using a Monte Carlo simulation of an MST design, they found that samples of 300 and 1,000 resulted in similar theta estimates and decision accuracies.

The commentary by Stark and Chernyshenko (2006/this issue) highlights some of the key findings of these articles, offers their perspective on the results, and makes suggestions about possible implications and future directions.

Taken as a group, these articles introduce the reader to practical aspects of MSTs and relate current knowledge of the practicality of different design and research decisions. These articles should prove interesting and helpful to psychometric researchers and practitioners interested in choosing between different test designs.

Finally, all of the research reported in these papers was initiated or funded as part of the American Institute for Certified Public Accountants (AICPA) Research Consortium. We gratefully acknowledge the support of the AICPA and the leadership of Craig Mills, Gerald Melican, and Krista Breithaupt.

REFERENCES

Chuah, S. C., Drasgow, F., & Luecht, R. (2006/this issue). How big is big enough? Sample size requirements for CAST item parameter estimation. *Applied Measurement in Education, 19,* 241–255.

Hambleton, R. K., & Xing, D. (2006/this issue). Optimal and nonoptimal computer-based test designs for making pass–fail decisions. *Applied Measurement in Education, 19,* 221–239.

Jodoin, M. G., Zenisky, A., & Hambleton, R. (2006/this issue). Comparison of the psychometric properties of several computer-based test designs for credentialing exams with multiple purposes. *Applied Measurement in Education, 19,* 203–220.

Lord, F. M. (1971). The self-scoring flexilevel test. *Journal of Educational Measurement, 8,* 147–151.

Lord, F. M. (1980). *Applications of item response theory to practical testing problems.* Hillsdale, NJ: Lawrence Erlbaum Associates, Inc.

Luecht, R., Brumfield, T., & Breithaupt, K. (2006/this issue). A testlet assembly design for adaptive multistage tests. *Applied Measurement in Education, 19,* 189–202.

Stark, S., & Chernyshenko, O. S. (2006/this issue). Multistage testing: Widely or narrowly applicable? *Applied Measurement in Education, 19,* 257–260.

Wainer, H. (2000). CATs: Whither and whence. *Psicológica, 21,* 121–133.

Subscription Information: *Applied Measurement in Education* is published quarterly by Lawrence Erlbaum Associates, Inc., 10 Industrial Avenue, Mahwah, NJ 07430–2262. Subscriptions for Volume 19, 2006, are available only on a calendar-year basis.

Individual rates: **Print *Plus* Online:** $55.00 in US/Canada, $85.00 outside US/Canada. Institutional rates: **Print-Only:** $470.00 in-US/Canada, $500.00 outside US/Canada. **Online-Only:** $445.00 in US/Canada and outside US/Canada. **Print *Plus* Online:** $495.00 in US/Canada, $525.00 outside US/Canada. Visit LEA's Web site at http://www.erlbaum.com to view a free sample.

Order subscriptions through the Journal Subscription Department, Lawrence Erlbaum Associates, Inc., 10 Industrial Avenue, Mahwah, NJ 07430–2262.

Address changes should include the mailing label or a facsimile. Claims for missing issues cannot be honored beyond 4 months after mailing date. Duplicate copies cannot be sent to replace issues not delivered due to failure to notify publisher of change of address.

This journal is abstracted or indexed in *PsycINFO/Psychological Abstracts; EBSCOhost Products; Contents Pages in Education; ISA; ISI: Current Contents/Social & Behavioral Sciences, Social Sciences Citation Index, Research Alert, Social SciSearch; Social Research Methodology; Education Index; Education Abstracts; Cabell's Directories.*

Microform copies of this journal are available through ProQuest Information and Learning, P.O. Box 1346, Ann Arbor, MI 48106–1346. For more information, call 1-800-521-0600, extension 2888.

APPLIED MEASUREMENT IN EDUCATION, *19*(3), 189–202

RESEARCH ARTICLES

A Testlet Assembly Design for Adaptive Multistage Tests

Richard Luecht and Terry Brumfield

Department of Educational Research Methodology
University of North Carolina at Greensboro

Krista Breithaupt

American Institute of Certified Public Accountants
Ewing, New Jersey

This article describes multistage tests and some practical test development considerations related to the design and implementation of a multistage test, using the Uniform CPA (certified public accountant) Examination as a case study. The article further discusses the use of automated test assembly procedures in an operational context to produce large numbers of adaptive testlets over time.

This article describes a multistage, computer-adaptive testlet examination administration format. Using the Uniform CPA (certified public accountant) Examination as a case study, some practical test development considerations related to the design and implementation of multistage tests are then described. The use of automated test assembly (ATA) procedures is also discussed in an operational context to produce large numbers of adaptive testlets over time.

The American Institute of Certified Public Accountants (AICPA) prepares the Uniform CPA (certified public accountant) Examination, the licensing examination used by 54 licensing jurisdictions to grant entry into the CPA profession. The AICPA has recently launched a computerized Uniform CPA Examination. This

Correspondence should be addressed to Richard Luecht, Department of Educational Research Methodology, University of North Carolina at Greensboro, P.O. Box 26170, Greensboro, NC 27402-6170. E-mail: rmluecht@uncg.edu conversion to computer-based testing included an extensive research agenda. This article focuses on one aspect of that agenda.

In its paper-and-pencil format, the Uniform CPA Examination had four sections: (a) audit, (b) accounting and reporting, (c) financial accounting and reporting, and (d) legal and professional responsibilities. Examinees typically took the four paper-and-pencil sections over a 2-day period (15.5 hr). The computerized examination has some perceptible changes in format and content, and a reduction in the total testing time.

Based on an extensive practice analysis of the CPA profession (Norris, Russell, Goodwin, & Jesse, 2001) and related research conducted by the AICPA, the new computerized examination differs from its predecessor in three ways. First, the content blueprint for the examination was reorganized and revised to emphasize four new areas: (a) audit and attestation, (b) financial accounting and reporting, (c) taxation and government regulations, and (d) business environment. Second, the skills measured by the examination were expanded to include written communications, integrated financial and accounting analysis tasks, and research. The addition of performance-based accounting simulations that incorporate features such as word processing, spreadsheet functionality, and online capabilities to search the authoritative accounting literature have made measurement of these additional skills possible (Devore, 2002). Third, the new examination uses adaptive testing technology to allow the examination to be shortened.

These changes in the Uniform CPA Examination had some obvious implications for test design and development. This article describes the resulting design in terms of two key issues: (a) the use of multistage adaptive *testlets*[1] to improve the efficiency of the examination and (b) the use of ATA procedures to produce large quantities of high-quality testlets that meet the Uniform CPA Examination specifications.

THE MULTISTAGE ADAPTIVE TESTLET
DELIVERY MODEL

In an extensive research effort over several years, the AICPA explored various test delivery models for the computerized Uniform CPA Examination. This research considered a wide range of operational, financial, and psychometric criteria. The test delivery models under consideration ranged from fixed test forms to content-balanced, computer-adaptive tests. For a variety of operational, security, and psychometric reasons, one of the more promising configurations that emerged was a three-stage, adaptive testlet delivery model. Luecht (2000) termed this type of de-

---

[1]Luecht and Nungester (1998) called the collection of items at each stage a *module* to avoid other connotations of the term *testlet*. In this article, the terms *testlet* and *module* are considered to be synonymous.

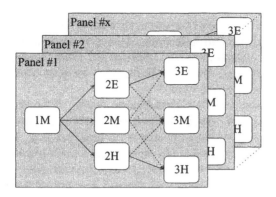

FIGURE 1   Design for a 1-3-3 computer adaptive sequential test configuration with multiple panels. E = relatively easy; M = moderately difficult; H = relatively hard.

livery model a *1-3-3 module* computer adaptive sequential test (CAST) configuration.[2] The CAST configuration is depicted in Figure 1.

The seven testlets shown on each of the gray rectangles in Figure 1 jointly represent a three-stage test in which the examinee gets only one of the available testlets per stage. Reading from left to right, there is one testlet assigned to the first stage (1M), three testlets assigned to the second stage (2E, 2M, and 2H), and three testlets assigned to the third stage (3E, 3M, and 3H); thus the label *1-3-3 CAST configuration*. The letters *E*, *M*, and *H* denote the average difficulty of the testlet (E = relatively easy, M = moderately difficult, H = relatively hard).

The possible routes through the seven testlets are indicated by the solid and dashed lines. Solid lines are used for the primary pathways (i.e., those routes most likely to be taken by examinees who perform as expected). Dashed lines denote the less common secondary pathways. For example, the centermost pathway would include the following sequence of testlets: 1M → 2M → 3M. Note that some pathways are precluded (e.g., an examinee would not be able to move from testlet 2E to 3H). Extreme changes in ability are unlikely by chance, and such unexpected performance would probably be flagged as aberrant. This configuration implements a policy to eliminate that possibility.

The seven testlets and the associated routing rules are packaged together in units called *panels* (Luecht & Nungester, 1998). Figure 1 depicts multiple panels (Panel #1, Panel #2, ... Panel #x). These multiple panels can be randomly assigned to examinees just like multiple test forms.

Each panel is uniquely defined and has its own identification number in the database. Every panel also contains seven different testlets, with each testlet assigned

---

[2]The operational CPA examination uses a simpler 1-2-2 design for reasons specific to the AICPA implementation.

exactly to one and only one of the seven positions within the panel. A specific set of routing rules also needs to be determined based on the particular statistical characteristics of the seven testlets that comprise the panel (scoring panels are described in a later section). Panels can be randomly assigned to examinees just like randomly assigned fixed test forms.

Numerous factors affect the measurement quality of the testlets within each panel and the scores that result from this type of multistage adaptive testlet design. For example, the size and characteristics of the item bank (e.g., the distribution of item difficulty and discrimination by content) has a direct impact on the possible breadth of test information that can be spread across the ability scale (i.e., there will be regions on the proficiency scale that will have limited test information due to limitations based on the size and characteristics of the item bank). The number of items per stage (testlet size) can directly affect the capability of the panel to adapt to examinees having more extreme abilities. Moreover, the testlet size per stage has a direct impact on the number of items needed per panel. This, of course, affects overall exposure risks by possibly limiting the number of panels that can be constructed from a finite item bank.

Table 1 shows 10 different specifications for a three-stage panel with the testlets ranging in size from 15 to 30 items. Each set of specifications assumes seven testlets and a total test length of 60 items (i.e., Stage 1 + Stage 2 + Stage 3 = 60 items). The leftmost three columns show the actual testlet size per stage. The next three columns show the total number of items required per stage for the 1-3-3 CAST panel configuration. For example, referring to the first data row in the table, the testlet sizes are 15, 15, and 30. The total numbers of items per stage are: (a) 15 × 1 = 15 at Stage 1, (b) 15 × 3 = 45 at Stage 2, and (c) 30 × 3 = 90 at Stage 3. The

TABLE 1
Panel Size as a Function of Testlet Size
(1-3-3 Computer Adapted Sequential Test Configuration)

Testlet Size Per Stage			Item Counts Per Stage			Total Panel Item Count
Stage 1	Stage 2	Stage 3	Stage 1	Stage 2	Stage 3	
15	15	30	15	45	90	150
20	15	25	20	45	75	140
25	15	20	25	45	60	130
30	15	15	30	45	45	120
15	20	25	15	60	75	150
20	20	20	20	60	60	140
25	20	15	25	60	45	130
15	25	20	15	75	60	150
20	25	15	20	75	45	140
15	30	15	15	90	45	150

rightmost column shows the total panel size (i.e., the total number of items needed to build the panel). For the first row, the total is $15 + 45 + 90 = 150$ items. Only multiples of five are shown for the testlet sizes (15, 20, 25, and 30 items).

It should be apparent from Table 1 that putting fewer items in the later stages has some obvious benefits in terms of minimizing the total number of items required per panel. Luecht and Nungester (1998) discussed how using smaller testlets in later stages also tended to allow test developers to better target the information provided by some of the latter-stage testlets toward the extremes of the ability distribution (subject, of course, to the availability of items in the item bank).

One implication of reducing the total number of items needed per panel is that we can correspondingly reduce certain types of item exposure risks. That is, given an item bank of fixed size, more panels can be created if fewer items are needed, overall, per panel. Increasing the number of available panels, in turn, reduces certain exposure risks due to concerted efforts by examinees to memorize test materials (Luecht, 1998b). For example, using the counts in Table 1, an item bank of 1,000 items could produce 6 to 8 unique panels. Ten to 12 panels could be built from a 1,500-item bank, and 13 to 16 panels could be created from an item bank containing 2,000 items. Of course, allowing systematic, controlled item overlap among different panels or even within panels would further increase the viable number of panels. (Items in testlets within the same level may overlap because an examinee sees only one testlet per stage.)

Scoring Panels

One advantage of packaging the testlets and routing rules together as a panel is that scoring can be simplified in terms of needed data and computational scoring functionality required by the test delivery computer software. Three types of scoring are needed for this type of multistage adaptive test: (a) scoring of the individual items, (b) cumulative scoring of the testlets for purposes of adaptively selecting the testlets in the subsequent stage, and (c) final scoring for purposes of reporting a score and making the associated pass–fail decision. The last type of scoring is not a concern in terms of what happens at the test center, provided that accurate data are captured and stored.

Real-time scoring by the test delivery software is required to allow a panel to adapt its testlets to an examinee's proficiency. Although item response theory (IRT) scoring (maximum likelihood or Bayes estimation) is certainly possible, Luecht and Nungester (1998) empirically demonstrated that number-correct scoring is probably sufficiently accurate for purposes of selecting testlets. Number-correct scoring simplifies the amount of data needed at the test center, complexity of scoring, and testlet selection routines that need to be supported by the test delivery software.

The basic implementation of number-correct scoring in this type of multistage adaptive test is to incrementally compute the upper and lower bounds for the number-correct scores associated with various combinations of testlets that reflect a particular routing decision to the next stage. For example, in adaptively transitioning from Stage 1 to Stage 2 in Panel #001 (Figure 1), we would need to know three pairs of values, corresponding to the upper and lower number-correct scores on Testlet 1M: $[X_{L(1)}, X_{U(1)}]$ to move to Testlet 2E, $[X_{L(2)}, X_{U(2)}]$ to move to Testlet 2M, and $[X_{L(3)}, X_{U(3)}]$ to move to 2H. Because examinees cannot score below zero or above the maximum possible points, we can set the lower bound for the easy route at $X_{L(1)} = 0$ and the upper bound for the hard route at $X_{U(3)} = n_j$, where n_j is the size (or maximum possible points) for the testlet. Using the lower and upper boundary pairs of values generalizes the selection routine.

Table 2 shows a sample routing data table for two panels, P1 and P2. This type of table could be stored in a database and would include all of the score routing information for all active panels. Optionally, separate tables could be created for each panel.

TABLE 2
A Sample Routing Table for Two Panels, P1 and P2

Panel ID	Current Stage	Route ID	Testlet History	Lower X_U	Upper X_U	Select Next Testlet
P1	1	R01		0	0	1
P1	2	R02	1	0	6	2
P1	2	R03	1	7	13	3
P1	2	R04	1	14	20	4
P1	3	R05	1,2	0	15	5
P1	3	R06	1,2	16	26	6
P1	3	R07	1,3	7	13	5
P1	3	R08	1,3	14	26	6
P1	3	R09	1,3	27	33	7
P1	3	R10	1,4	14	23	6
P1	3	R11	1,4	24	40	7
P1	1	R12		0	20	1
P2	2	R13	1	0	6	2
P2	2	R14	1	7	13	3
P2	2	R15	1	14	20	4
P2	3	R16	1,2	0	15	5
P2	3	R17	1,2	16	26	6
P2	3	R18	1,3	7	13	5
P2	3	R19	1,3	14	26	6
P2	3	R20	1,3	27	33	7
P2	3	R21	1,4	14	23	6
P2	3	R22	1,4	24	40	7

Panel ID is included for look-up purposes. Current Stage is the present state of the test (e.g., 1 indicates that a testlet for Stage 1 must be selected). The Testlet History column contains a comma-delimited string of integers that identifies the previously administered testlets within the panel. The testlets are indexed by the integers 1, 2, 3, ... 7, where 1 = Testlet 1M, 2 = Testlet 2E, 3 = Testlet 2M, 4 = Testlet 2H, 5 = Testlet 3E, 6 = Testlet 3M, and 7 = Testlet 3H. For example, a testlet history of 1,3 indicates that testlets 1M and 2M have been administered through the second stage of testing. The score for the previously administered testlets is used for the adaptive routing decision to the next testlet. The Lower X_L and Upper X_U columns contain the upper and lower bounds for the adaptive selection. When the current score satisfies $X_L \leq X \leq X_U$, the score routing rule fires as "true," and the testlet in the Select Next Testlet column is given. As before, the integers 1 to 7 denote the seven testlets in each panel.

IRT is used to determine the proficiency estimates. We start by locating one or more points on the proficiency scale, θ_d, each of which corresponds to a particular decision point for routing examinees (i.e., for choosing between which of two possible testlets to administer next). For example, given Testlet 1M, we need to decide between Testlet 2E and 2M (easy vs. moderate) or between Testlet 2M and 2H (moderate vs. hard). Given a particular decision point, θ_d, and the IRT item parameters for a set of k testlets administered up to that point, ξ_i, $i = 1, ..., n_j, j = 1, ..., k$, the corresponding estimated true-score point is

$$X_d = \sum_{j=1}^{k} \sum_{i=1}^{n_j} P(\theta_d ; \xi_i),$$

where $P(\theta_d, \xi_i)$ is the item response function for a particular IRT model. The computed value can be rounded to approximate a number-correct integer score, if needed.

All of these computations are done for each panel before it is released for use. Once the number-correct routing scores are determined for a panel, the IRT data are no longer needed. A number-correct scoring function, the routing table, and a simple look-up mechanism are sufficient to allow each panel to adapt itself.

There are (at least) two methods for locating the routing points on the ability scale. The approximate maximum information (AMI) method empirically determines the cut point(s) using the cumulative test information function for the previously administered testlets and the testlets at the current stage. This method mimics an adaptive test by choosing the testlet likely to provide maximum information about an examinee, given a current provisional score.

Under the AMI method, the cumulative test information functions (TIFs) are evaluated pairwise for adjacent testlets within each panel. The AMI method finds the optimal decision point on the θ scale for selecting between two testlets, using a maximum-information criterion similar to any computerized adaptive test. That is, the intersection of the TIFs corresponds to the decision point insofar as selecting one or the other testlet. This intersection is relatively easy to find using standard numerical analysis root-finding techniques (e.g., using numerical bisection to find the value of θ at which the information functions are equal because they intersect with one another). For example, assuming the administration of testlet 1M in Panel #001 (see Figure 1), we would like to find two routing points: θ_1, corresponding to the intersection of the TIF curves $I(1M + 2E) \cap I(1M + 2M)$, and θ_2, corresponding to the intersection of the TIF curves $I(1M + 2M) \cap I(1M + 2H)$.

Once we locate those two points, we can compute the corresponding estimated true-score values on the test characteristic surface for testlet 1M; that is, we compute

$$X_1 = \sum_{i \in 1M} P(\theta_1; \xi_i) \text{ and } X_2 = \sum_{i \in 1M} P(\theta_2; \xi_i).$$

This process of determining the score routing points can be repeated for each of the possible routes in the panel. The results can be then be tabled and packaged as part of the panel data. Note that the routing points, θ_1 and θ_2, and the approximate number-correct cut points, X_1 and X_2, will probably differ from testlet to testlet, unless the TIFs and associated test characteristic curves for the replicated testlets on multiple panels are virtually identical.

A second method of determining cut points is the *defined population intervals* method. This method can be used to implement a policy that specifies the relative proportions of examinees in the population expected to follow each of the three primary routes through the panel. For example, if we determine, as a matter of policy, that we want approximately equal proportions of examines in the population exposed to the three primary pathways in our 1-3-3 panel (i.e., 1M + 2E + 3E, 1M + 2M + 3M, and 1M + 2H + 3H), we could find the ability scores associated with the 33rd and 67th percentiles of the cumulative distribution of θ. Assuming θ to be normally distributed ($\mu = 0$, $\sigma^2 = 1$) the routing points would be $\theta_1 = -0.44$ and $\theta_2 = 0.44$, which can easily be verified from a standard table of values for the unit normal distribution. The approximate number-correct routing scores could then be determined as outlined previously for the AMI method.

It should be clear that when a particular panel is selected, all of the information needed to administer the testlets and items for that panel is contained (directly or by reference) within the panel "wrapper." In addition to facilitating quality assurance, the panel concept also allows panels to be blocked for certain examinees (e.g., in cases of retesting, previously seen panels can be blocked, including other panels with substantial numbers of overlapping items).

USING ATA TO CONSTRUCT PANELS

ATA involves the use of mathematical optimization procedures to select items from an item bank for one or more test forms, subject to multiple constraints related to the content and other qualitative features. van der Linden (1998) presented an excellent overview of the most popular ATA heuristics and mathematical programming techniques.

A simple example may help for purposes of illustration. We start by specifying a quantity to minimize or maximize. This quantity is called the *objective function* and can be formulated as a mathematical function to be optimized by linear programming algorithms or heuristics. *Constraints* are imposed on the solution, usually reflecting the content blueprint or other qualitative features of the items that we wish to control (e.g., word counts). The constraints are typically expressed as equalities (exact numbers of items to select) or inequalities (upper or lower bounds on the number of items to select).

For example, suppose that we want to maximize the IRT test information at a fixed cut point, denoted θ_0, with a fixed test length of 20 items. We need to define a binary decision variable, x_i, $i = 1, \ldots I$ that indicates item i is selected ($x_i = 1$) or not ($x_i = 0$) from the item bank. Given this decision variable, the objective function to be maximized is the IRT test information function for the selected items; that is,

$$I(\theta_0) = \sum_{i=1}^{I} I(\theta_0, \xi_i) x_i \qquad (1)$$

where ξ_i denotes the item parameters from the item bank ($i = 1, \ldots I$; e.g., $\xi_i = [a_i, b_i, c_i]$ for the three-parameter logistic model). Now, suppose we have two content areas, C_1 and C_2, and wish to have at least 5 items from content area C_1 and no more than 10 items from content area C_2. This ATA problem can be modeled as follows:

maximize $\qquad \sum_{i=1}^{I} I(\theta_0, \xi_i) x_i \qquad$ (maximum information) $\qquad (2)$

subject to:

$$\sum_{i \in C_1}^{I} x_i \geq 5 \qquad \text{(constraint on } C_1) \qquad (3)$$

$$\sum_{i \in C_2}^{I} x_i \leq 10 \qquad \text{(constraint on } C_2) \qquad (4)$$

$$\sum_{i=1}^{I} x_i = 10 \qquad \text{(test length)} \qquad (5)$$

$$x_i \in (0, 1), i = 1, \ldots, I. \qquad \text{(range of variables)} \qquad (6)$$

It is relatively straightforward to extend these basic ATA procedures to a multistage adaptive testlet environment like CAST (Luecht, 2000). For the type of ATA problem implied by the CAST model described in the previous section, it is useful to use what Luecht (2000) called the *bottom-up* CAST design strategy. This bottom-up strategy essentially treats the test assembly process as a simultaneous, multiple-objective function optimization problem in which we are simultaneously building one or more versions of seven different tests (i.e., the seven testlets in each panel). Accordingly, implementing this approach requires separate test specifications (statistical targets and content constraints) for each testlet.

Specific to the 1-3-3 CAST panel design shown in Figure 1, we need to specify seven independent test information function targets, where the TIF was given in Equation 1. That is, we must specify seven unique TIF targets at multiple θ values, approximating seven TIF target curves.

Figure 2 shows a conceptual picture of seven target information function curves, each corresponding to one of the testlet positions shown in Figure 1. The location of the peak of the TIF curve for each target can vary within and across stages, corresponding to desired changes in the average difficulty of the testlets. The amount of information targeted per testlet may also vary depending on the testing stage and the availability of informative items in the item bank.

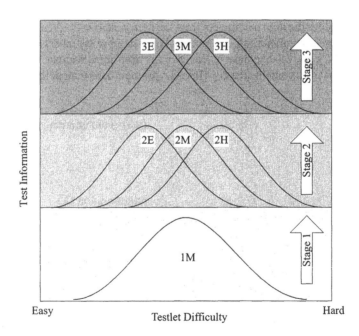

FIGURE 2   Seven target testlet information functions for the 1-3-3 computer adaptive sequential test configuration. E = relatively easy; M = moderately difficult; H = relatively hard.

In addition to statistical specifications, separate content specifications are required for each of the three stages; that is, there will be one set of content specifications for Stage 1, representing the content requirements for Testlet 1M. There will be a second set of content specifications for the three Stage 2 testlets (2E, 2M, and 2H). The implication is that although those three testlets will be targeted to have different statistical characteristics, they are required to meet the same content specifications within Stage 2. Similarly, a third set of content specifications is required for the three testlets at the third stage (3E, 3M, and 3H). If content were not able to be allocated to the individual stages, then the bottom-up strategy could not be used (Luecht, 2000; Luecht & Nungester, 1998).

Finally, we need to specify the length of each testlet and content requirements for each stage in the panel. If the four CPA examination sections are, on average, 60 items in length, with 15 to 25 items per any stage, then under the bottom-up CAST assembly strategy each of the seven testlets per panel can be treated as a separate test assembly project of approximately 20 items.

These specifications will be used to simultaneously solve seven optimization models, one for each testlet position in the panel (see Figure 1), and produce multiple parallel versions of each testlet. Once we have the multiple replications of the seven testlets we can assemble them, by any number of viable combinatoric means,[3] to create different versions of the panels. The unique list of constructed testlets, their assignments to the pathways and stages within each panel, and the associated scoring and routing rules can then be packaged as part of each panel.

A somewhat minor challenge remains in simultaneously solving seven optimization models. That is, we need to devise and solve an ATA model that allows us to simultaneously build multiple replications of the seven individual testlets: 1M, 2E, 2M, 2H, 3E, 3M, and 3H (see Figure 1), each meeting a potentially different set of statistical and content constraints. In theory, this type of problem can be readily solved using dedicated ATA optimization heuristics (Luecht, 1998a; Luecht & Nungester, 1998). However, working computer software that implements this type of 1-3-3 CAST model using a bottom-up strategy has not yet been completed, and preexisting CAST test assembly software is not particularly useful for this application. The Appendix presents an algorithm that a new ATA software engine, currently under construction, will use. This algorithm is based on Luecht's (1998a) normalized weighted absolute deviation heuristic.

An alternative (currently used with the CPA examination), is linear programming. An ATA approach based on linear programming provides more exact results than heuristics (van der Linden, 1998). Solving this type of multitarget problem with linear programming is somewhat challenging—but not insurmountable. The

---

[3]Overlap among the panels can be explicitly handled by means of overlapping testlets. Exposure risks for individual testlets and panels can be analytically computed or approximated by using simulated response data, based on characteristics of the target population.

AICPA uses CPLEX (ILOG, 2002), a software suite that conveniently handles large-scale optimization problems using the branch-and-bound algorithms and requisite relaxation techniques to deal with infeasibilities in the linear programming solution (see, e.g., Timminga, 1998).

CONCLUSIONS

Adaptive multistage testing frameworks such as CAST have some distinct advantages over conventional fixed-form computer-based testing and even computerized adaptive testing in terms of control over test assembly and test form quality control, exposure of test materials, facilitating data management, and reducing the requirements for test delivery software to handle complex scoring and item selection algorithms. This article has presented a particular CAST design: the 1-3-3 panel design.

There are remaining issues to resolve. These issues include deciding on the optimal number of stages and range of testlet difficulty within stages, deriving feasible statistical information targets to address psychometric as well as exposure concerns, carrying out research on the differences between scores and decisions based on number-correct score routing versus using IRT score routing, and understanding the limitations of various ATA approaches for building multistage tests.

ACKNOWLEDGMENTS

We thank the American Institute of Certified Public Accountants for their support of this research, especially Alan Mead, Gerald Melican, and Craig Mills. In addition, we are indebted to Ronald Hambleton and Wim van der Linden for their insights on various technical aspects of this work.

REFERENCES

Devore, R. (2002, April). *Considerations in the development of accounting simulations.* Paper presented at the annual meeting of the National Council on Measurement in Education, New Orleans, LA.

ILOG, Inc. (2005). CPLEX Suite (Version 9.1) [Computer software]. Mountain View, CA: Author.

Luecht, R. M. (1998a). Computer-assisted test assembly using optimization heuristics. *Applied Psychological Measurement, 22,* 224–236.

Luecht, R. M. (1998b, April). *A framework for exploring and controlling risks associated with test item exposure over time.* Paper presented at the annual meeting of the National Council in Measurement in Education, San Diego, CA.

Luecht, R. M. (2000, April). *Implementing the Computer-Adaptive Sequential Testing (CAST) Framework to mass produce high quality computer-adaptive and mastery tests.* Paper presented at the annual meeting of the National Council on Measurement in Education, New Orleans, LA.

Luecht, R. M., & Nungester, R. (1998). Some practical examples of computer-adaptive sequential testing. *Journal of Educational Measurement, 35,* 229–249.

Norris, D. G., Russell, T. L., Goodwin, G. F., & Jesse, C. L, (2001). *Practice analysis of certified public accountants: Technical report.* Jersey City, NJ: American Institute of Certified Public Accountants.

Timminga, E. (1998). Solving infeasibility problems in computerized test assembly. *Applied Psychological Measurement, 22,* 280–291.

van der Linden, W. J. (1998). Optimal assembly of psychological and educational tests. *Applied Psychological Measurement, 22,* 195–211.

APPENDIX
An Algorithm for Multitarget Bundling
With Automated Test Assembly

Set-ups

1. Assumption: There is a single item bank (database) containing item statistics and attributes (e.g., content codes).
2. The fundamental unit for test assembly is called a *bundle*. Each *bundle* can represent a testlet, a fixed test form, or a combination of several testlets. Each bundle has a fixed has a set of attribute constraints to control the distribution of content and other categorical features, as well as a specific set of statistical targets (e.g., test information values at a fixed number of θ points).
   a. The attribute constraints can be different for different bundles.
   b. The targets can be different for different bundles.
3. Bundles can be replicated.

Processing

1. The item bank file, the attribute constraints file(s), and the statistical target file (containing multiple targets) are input to the automated test assembly software.
2. J bundles are indexed to constraint files and to statistical target fields (e.g., columns, with θ values as rows for test information targets).
3. Item selection tables are created for each replicate of every bundle—the total number of tables is $h = \Sigma r(j)$, where $r(j)$ is the number of replications of bundle j ($j = 1, \ldots J$). $S(k)$ indexes the tables, $k = 1, \ldots, h$.

Algorithm

1. Select a bundle replicate at random.
2. Build the necessary normalized weighted absolute deviation heuristic indexes and temporary arrays
3. Choose *one* item via the normalized weighted absolute deviation heuristic (Luecht, 1998) for that bundle table, $S(k)$.
4. Select another bundle.
5. Repeat Step 3. Continue until one item has been selected for all bundle replicates.
6. Free all bundles to be selected with equal probability.
7. Go to Step 1 and repeat until all bundle tables are full.

APPLIED MEASUREMENT IN EDUCATION, *19*(3), 203–220

Comparison of the Psychometric Properties of Several Computer-Based Test Designs for Credentialing Exams With Multiple Purposes

Michael G. Jodoin
Educational Testing Service
Princeton, New Jersey

April Zenisky and Ronald K. Hambleton
Center for Educational Assessment
University of Massachusetts, Amherst

Many credentialing agencies today are either administering their examinations by computer or are likely to be doing so in the coming years. Unfortunately, although several promising computer-based test designs are available, little is known about how well they function in examination settings. The goal of this study was to compare fixed-length examinations (both operational forms and newly constructed forms) with several variations of multistage test designs for making pass–fail decisions. Results were produced for 3 passing scores. Four operational 60-item examinations were compared to (a) 3 new 60-item forms, (b) 60-item 3-stage tests, and (c) 40-item 2-stage tests; all were constructed using automated test assembly software. The study was carried out using computer simulation techniques that were set to mimic common examination practices. All 60-item tests, regardless of design or passing score, produced accurate ability estimates and acceptable and similar levels of decision consistency and decision accuracy. One interesting finding was that the 40-item test results were poorer than the 60-item test results, as expected, but were in the range of acceptability. This raises the practical policy question of whether content-valid 40-item tests with lower item exposure levels and/or savings in item development costs are an acceptable trade-off for a small loss in decision accuracy and consistency.

Correspondence should be addressed to Michael G. Jodoin, Educational Testing Service, MS 03-T Rosedale Road, Princeton NJ 08541. E-mail: mjodoin@ets.org

Many credentialing examination boards today are either administering their examinations via computer or expect to be doing so within the next few years. There are many well-known reasons for credentialing examinations to switch their examinations from paper-and-pencil to computer-based administrations. For example, powerful incentives to move to computer-based administrations include the flexibility for candidates to schedule their exams at convenient times; availability of immediate score reporting; and potentially improving validity through the introduction of new item formats that are more closely aligned with the knowledge, skills, and abilities of interest. Of course, there are potentially negative consequences of computer-administered examinations as well. For example, there is an increased threat of item compromise because examinations are typically being administered more frequently. This may result in substantially increased item development requirements with associated costs passed on to candidates (e.g., Mills, Potenza, Fremer, & Ward, 2002; van der Linden & Glas, 2000; Wainer, 2000). Regardless of these and other shortcomings, the transition of credentialing exams from paper-and-pencil administrations to computer-based administrations seems inevitable.

COMPUTER-BASED TEST DESIGNS

Once the decision has been made to computerize the administration of an examination, several test-design options that differentially constrain the level of test individualization are readily available. At one end of the continuum reflecting the extent to which a computer-based exam adapts item selection to the performance of candidates during an examination administration is a *linear fixed-length test* (LFT). Here, separate test forms are assembled in their entirety so that they are closely matched to each other in content and item statistics. These forms can be assigned on a random basis to candidates, and the number of fixed test forms that are available can control the exposure level of individual test items. This format provides the most control in test design because each form can be carefully inspected and reviewed before administration. A popular variation on fixed-form examinations is a *linear on-the-fly test* (LOFT), in which each candidate receives a unique set of test items that is matched to content and statistical specifications. This variation, however, provides less control than a LFT design because forms are dynamically created via an algorithm immediately prior to each administration and consequently it does not allow for inspection and review by test developers. For LOFT designs, item exposure levels become more complex as higher levels of item overlap are likely with the large number of unique forms typical of LOFT designs. Both LFT and LOFT designs are nonadaptive because all items are selected before a candidate has been administered an exam.

At the other end of the test adaptation continuum is a *computerized adaptive test* (CAT). Here, content specifications remain essential, and items are selected to optimize the measurement properties of the test administered to each candidate subject to content specifications. A variety of stopping rules for the examination are available, including achieving a desired level of measurement error or achieving a desired level of decision accuracy (e.g., .90 probability of a correct decision). Item exposure can be controlled overall or made conditional on ability (e.g., Stocking & Lewis, 2000). This test design provides the least control for test developers because each test form is dynamically created by an algorithm that selects items one at a time, on the basis of the most recent proficiency estimate for a candidate, during administration. Although expected test forms can be simulated and reviewed by test developers, actual test forms cannot be inspected or reviewed until after the test administration is complete. However, CAT administration provides the highest levels of precision because there are more opportunities to adapt the test to candidate proficiency.

In the middle of the test adaptation continuum is a *multistage test* (MST). Using the nomenclature developed by Luecht and Nungester (1998), test items are administered to candidates in series of fixed sets of items, called *modules* (also called *item blocks* or *testlets*). A test form consists of a series of *stages* in which one or more modules are administered. Adaptation may occur between each stage by selecting tailored modules that are matched to the proficiency estimate of the candidate from the items included in all previously administered modules. Figure 1 provides an example of a three-stage MST. All candidates are given a module of moderate difficulty in Stage 1. Subsequently, a proficiency estimate is computed based on the items in Stage 1, and weak, average, and strong

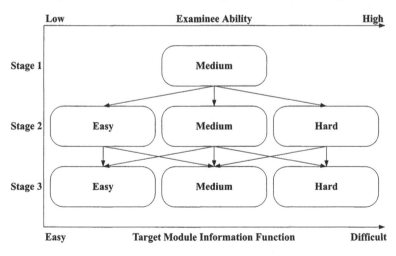

FIGURE 1   A three-stage multistage test design.

candidates are administered easy, moderate, and difficult modules, respectively. Next, another proficiency estimate is computed on the basis of the items administered in all previous stages (i.e., Stages 1 and 2) and candidates are administered a module of appropriate difficulty in Stage 3. This process could be generalized to MST designs that include more modules in each stage or more stages. In this regard, an n-stage MST in which each module consists of a single item is comparable to a CAT, and a one-stage MST with one n-item module is comparable to an LFT.

To control item exposure levels, multiple modules are assembled so that they are closely matched on content and statistical specifications. Then, MST *panels*, or test forms, are assembled so that each panel follows a common MST design, such as the one depicted in Figure 1, but contains a unique combination of modules. Thus, exposure can be controlled by randomly assigning candidates to panels, and the exposure for each module can be determined in advance, or at least predicted if a reasonably accurate estimate of the candidate score distribution is available. In addition, MST designs provide a relatively high level of control for test developers because each module and panel may be reviewed before administration.

MST designs possess other desirable characteristics. Candidates may change answers or skip test items and return to them prior to actually finishing a module and moving on to another. This limited control by the candidate (i.e., being able to omit test items and/or skip test items and return to them later) is a test administration feature that is responsive to one of the main criticisms of CAT administrations (Vispoel, 1998). Measurement precision may be gained over LFT or LOFT designs without an increase in test length by adapting the exam administration to the performance levels of the candidates (see, e.g., Lord, 1980; Patsula, 1999; Patsula & Hambleton, 1999). Of course, in practice MST designs have many degrees of freedom: They can vary in the numbers of modules that are administered, the lengths of modules, branching rules used, amount of item overlap in the modules, item exposure levels, and so on.

It is clear, then, that a number of computer-based test designs are available, and MST designs appear to be a promising alternative to LFT or CAT designs. However, additional research is needed and, perhaps surprisingly, given its potential for improving assessment practices, MST designs have received much less research attention than CAT designs. For example, only a few studies have considered the use of the MST design when classification of candidates is the main purpose of testing. For prominent exceptions, see Luecht and Nungester (1998) and several chapters in the edited book by van der Linden and Glas (2000).

A number of previous studies have compared computer-based test designs in terms of the reliability of ability estimates. Such studies are helpful, but they do not directly address the fundamental measurement problem with credentialing exams: to make reliable and valid pass–fail decisions. In principle, it is quite possible that a computer-based test design might lead to relatively poor ability estimates, although the test design may be quite acceptable for making sufficiently reliable and valid pass–fail decisions. This might be the case, for example, with fixed-form examinations that typically result in less-than-optimal estimation of low- and high-ability scores, but the level of precision achieved with this examination design may be sufficient for making reliable and valid pass–fail decisions (especially if the pass rate is somewhere in the middle of the candidate score distribution). Xing (2000) and Xing and Hambleton (2004) have compared computer-based test designs to investigate the reliability and validity of pass–fail decisions, but their primary variables of interest were item quality and item bank size.

Little research has compared test designs when an examination has multiple purposes. For example, credentialing tests may be primarily used in pass–fail decisions that necessitate high levels of decision accuracy at the pass score. However, secondary purposes, such as providing diagnostic reports for less proficient candidates, rewarding the highest-achieving examinees, and pass–fail decisions that are contingent on base performance levels on other subtests may require accurate measurement across a range on the proficiency scale. When both high decision accuracy and reliability are important goals, MST and CAT designs may be options preferable to LFT designs of the same length. However, when high levels of control are required by test developers to ensure rigorous control of all test forms, as in credentialing exams with high stakes, MST designs may hold significant advantages compared with CAT designs. Therefore, the purpose of this study was to compare LFT (both operational forms and newly constructed forms) with two MST designs in regard to decision accuracy and reliability.

METHOD

Data from four operational paper-and-pencil administrations of a large-scale, high-stakes, national certification examination, each consisting of approximately 60 dichotomously scored multiple-choice items classified into three main content areas, were used in the study. Historically, the operational test specifications allowed limited flexibility in the number of items from each content area but, for the purposes of this study, and to reflect a move toward a less flexible test blueprint, the mean number of items in each content area (across the four operational forms) was used as the content specification for the development of all subsequent forms in the study. Exam items were calibrated using the three-parameter item response theory model to develop an item bank that consisted of 238 items. These item parameter estimates were used for subsequent automated test forms assembly and for the simulation of candidate item response data.

To develop realistic target information functions for new fixed form and MST designs with the existing item bank, test information functions for each of the four operational forms were determined and are displayed in Figure 2. Subsequently, the mean of the four operational test information functions was used a basis for the

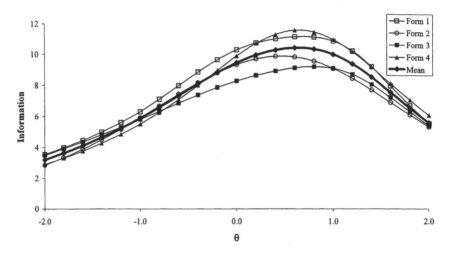

FIGURE 2   Operational form information functions.

development of target information functions for automated test assembly using CASTISEL (Luecht, 1996).

LFT Assembly

Three LFT forms consisting of 60 items each were created using the content specifications and the target information function. This resulted in three content-balanced 60-item test forms that will subsequently be referred to as *LFT Forms 1, 2*, and *3*, respectively, to distinguish them from the four operational (i.e., real) test forms. Three forms were generated because it would allow an item exposure rate of 33% and use three quarters of the available item pool. We felt that, given the size of the item pool, this reflected a reasonable compromise between item exposure and pool usage. In operational situations, a larger item pool and lower exposure controls would be needed. For example, doubling the item bank would enable twice as many nonoverlapping forms to be assembled and exposure level of items to be cut to 16.7%. Doubling the bank again could reduce item level exposure below 10%.

Figure 3 displays the test information functions for each LFT form and the target test information function. It is apparent from Figure 3 that the test forms assembled with CASTISEL provided less than the specified information for higher abilities and for two of the three forms more information at lower abilities.[1] These are

---

[1]The inability of CASTISEL to meet the test information target generated from the mean of the operational test forms while using only three quarters of the items is likely due to variability of the content specifications between operational forms. This had the effective result of placing tight content specifications on the test, given the item bank in this study.

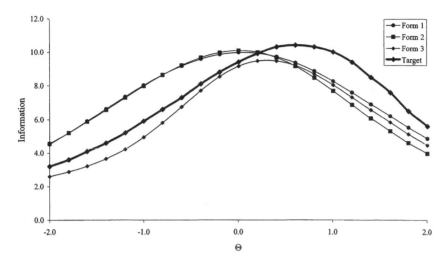

FIGURE 3   Linear fixed-length test information functions.

not ideal forms, but they represent the best that could be constructed with the available item bank, the content specifications, and the version of the test assembly software we were using at the time.

MST Assembly

Next, a three-stage MST design following a 1-3-3 stage structure was constructed as illustrated in Figure 1. Again, the mean test information function from the operational administrations was used to form target information functions for each module. Target information functions for the medium-difficulty modules for Stages 1, 2, and 3 were set to one third the value of the mean test information function from the operational forms. The easy modules in Stages 2 and 3 were set to one third of value of the mean test information function, with a negative horizontal transformation of one half a standard deviation. The hard modules in Stages 2 and 3 were set to one third of the value of the mean test information function with a positive horizontal transformation of one half a standard deviation. That is, the easy and hard modules were identical to the medium-difficulty module in terms of information but shifted left and right by one half a standard deviation, respectively.

To maintain an item exposure level of 33%, three modules were constructed for the medium-difficulty Stage 1 module. This made it possible to create three MST panels: Each MST panel consisted of one of the three unique Stage 1 medium difficulty modules and the same six modules in the second and third stages; the panels are referred to as Panels 1, 2, and 3. Thus, nine 20-item modules were simultaneously created, resulting in item pool usage and item exposure rates that would be comparable to the LFT condition. This three-stage MST design with module target information functions based on one third of the mean operational test information function is subsequently referred to as *3-Stage MST Design 1*. Figure 4 shows the module information functions for the first panel of the 3-Stage MST Design 1. Again, the automated test assembly process had difficulty meeting the target information for higher abilities but in general provided additional information at lower abilities.

Subsequently, a second three-stage MST with a 1-3-3 design was developed. In this MST design, target information functions for Stage 1 modules were reduced to one quarter, and Stage 2 and 3 modules were increased to three-eighths of the mean operational test information function. This design had the desirable effect of placing the more discriminating items in Stage 2 and 3 modules when better matching of candidate ability estimates and item difficulties is possible. The idea is simple: To gain an advantage from the most discriminating items, it is best to have good ability estimates for optimal assignment. More accurate ability estimates are available after the first and second stages than before the first stage is administered, and so moving the more discriminating items to the second and third stages of an MST should improve measurement precision.

Once again, easy and hard module target information functions were horizontally translated by one half a standard deviation to the left and right, respectively.

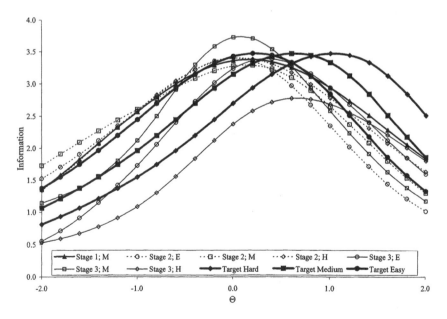

FIGURE 4   Module information functions, three-stage multistage test Design 1, Form 1. M = medium; E = easy; H = hard.

Similarly, three 20-item Stage 1 modules were created simultaneously with six 20-item Stage 2 and 3 modules to create three MST panels. This MST design is subsequently referred to as *3-Stage MST Design 2*. Although not shown, as in the Design 1 module, information functions are below the target information functions for higher abilities, reflecting the limited number of difficulty discriminating items in the item pool.

In preliminary analyses of both three-stage MST designs, ability estimates computed at the end of each stage in the three-stage design were correlated with the true ability for each MST panel for two replications and are summarized in Table 1. This analysis had a major implication for the design of the study. Although there was a substantial improvement in the ability estimates between the end of the first and second stages, the improvement between the second and third stages was somewhat modest. This result suggested that two additional MST test designs would be informative. A 2-Stage MST Design 1 was created by simply eliminating the Stage 3 modules from the 3-Stage MST Design 1. This resulted in a two-stage MST design with three panels. Each panel consisted of one of three unique 20-item medium-difficulty modules in the first stage and the same easy, medium, and hard modules in Stage 2 of the three-stage equivalent. Similarly, the 3-Stage MST Design 2 was converted to a *2-Stage MST Design 2* by simply dropping the Stage 3 modules. With these two additional designs, it was possible to compare 40-item and 60-item MST designs to each other and to the operational forms.

Data Generation

Using the item parameters from the large-sample three-parameter item response theory calibration of the operational forms, examinee response data for each Test Form × Test Design combination (four operational test forms; three LFT forms; three panels each of 3-Stage MST Design 1 and 2, and 2-Stage MST Design 1 and

TABLE 1
Correlations Between True and Estimated Ability by Stage
and by Replication for Three-Stage Multistage Test

| | Replication 1 | | | Replication 2 | | |
	Stage 1	*Stage 2*	*Stage 3*	*Stage 1*	*Stage 2*	*Stage 3*
Design 1						
Form 1	.840	.914	.935	.840	.915	.935
Form 2	.849	.916	.936	.850	.915	.936
Form 3	.844	.915	.936	.849	.915	.936
Design 2						
Form 1	.814	.913	.938	.814	.916	.938
Form 2	.809	.910	.937	.810	.911	.937
Form 3	.813	.911	.935	.817	.912	.937

2) were simulated using MSTSIM (Jodoin, 2002). For each test form, the identical random sample of 5,000 examinees from a normal distribution with mean of 0 and standard deviation of 1 was used to closely reflect the actual distribution of the examinee population. By using a very large examinee sample size, sampling errors in the statistics of interest could be kept very small, reducing problems in interpreting the main results.

For all analyses, maximum likelihood estimates were used for computing ability estimates (see Hambleton, Swaminathan, & Rogers, 1991; Lord, 1980). On the basis of ability estimates at the end of a previous stage, candidates were assigned to the easy and hard modules if their ability estimates were below −.43 and above .43, respectively, and to the medium module otherwise. This allocation plan ensured a common item exposure rate of approximately 33%. Also, pathways were restricted so that examinees were not able to move from easy to hard or from hard to easy modules in successive stages, because this would reflect an aberrant (i.e., non-model-fitting) behavior and in practice would be subject to review.[2]

To evaluate the accuracy of ability estimates from each test design, three correlation analyses were conducted. First, the correlations between the true ability and final ability estimates were computed for each replication of each test design by form. Second, test–retest reliability was computed by correlating the final ability estimates between two replications of the first form of each test design. Third, alternate-forms[3] reliability was computed by correlating the final ability estimates between each form within test design.

Although accurate ability estimates are generally important in testing, the primary indicators of reliability for a certification examination are the levels of decision accuracy and decision consistency that are achieved. To investigate the capabilities of each test design to properly classify examinees as qualified or unqualified candidates, analyses were conducted with pass rates of approximately 30%, 40%, and 50%. True and estimated abilities above .521, .223, and .000 were classified as true or observed certifiable candidates, and true and estimated abilities below these values were classified as true or observed noncertifiable candidates. The three pass rates span the range of pass rates that are expected with this credentialing agency. Furthermore, it should provide an important basis for generalizing the results of this study because the number of examinees near a passing score affects the decision consistency and decision accuracy.

To assess the capability of each test design to properly classify examinees as certifiable or noncertifiable, decision accuracy, false-positive and false-negative rates,

---

[2]In this study, this restriction was not required; no candidate had such drastic changes in ability estimates. This is likely the result of relatively long modules and item responses that were generated according to the model used in scoring.

[3]The term *alternate forms* is used loosely in this context for the MST designs. The alternate forms could potentially consist of a large number of the same items depending on the pathway taken by an examinee through each MST panel.

and kappa coefficients were calculated. Finally, the decision consistency and kappa coefficient were calculated by comparing the classification decisions for examinees on Forms 1 through 3 of each test design at each passing score. For both the decision accuracy and consistency analyses, results were reported for Replication 1 only. Similar findings were obtained with the additional forms and replications.

RESULTS

The correlations between the true and estimated ability scores are provided in Table 2. Clearly, all test designs performed comparably to the original four test forms. However, correlations were highest and most consistent across the real, LFT, and three-stage MST designs, ranging between .92 and .94. Although still large, the correlations for the two-stage MST designs were somewhat lower, on the magnitude of .91. In addition, no differences of note were obtained between MST Designs 1 and 2 in either the two- or three-stage MST designs.

Tables 3, 4, and 5 provide the test–retest and alternate-forms reliabilities for the LFT, three-stage, and two-stage MST designs, respectively. The alternate-form and

TABLE 2
Correlations Between True and Final Ability Estimates

Type	Form	Replication 1	Replication 2
Real	1	.937	.938
Real	2	.928	.932
Real	3	.931	.930
Real	4	.934	.933
LFT	1	.941	.938
LFT	2	.937	.936
LFT	3	.927	.922
3-Stage MST			
Design 1	1	.935	.935
Design 1	2	.936	.936
Design 1	3	.936	.936
Design 2	1	.938	.938
Design 2	2	.937	.937
Design 2	3	.935	.937
2-Stage MST			
Design 1	1	.915	.914
Design 1	2	.916	.918
Design 1	3	.916	.913
Design 2	1	.917	.912
Design 2	2	.916	.910
Design 2	3	.913	.911

Note.   LFT = linear fixed-length test; MST = multistage test.

TABLE 3
Test–Retest and Alternate Form Reliability
Estimates for Linear Fixed-Length Test (LFT)

	LFT Form		
	1	2	3
Form 1	.878	.881	.869
Form 2		.878	.867
Form 3			.856

Note. Alternate form reliabilities are based on Replication 1.

TABLE 4
Test–Retest and Alternate Form Reliability Estimates
for a Three-Stage Multistage Test

	Design 1			Design 2		
	1	2	3	1	2	3
Form 1	.875	.872	.876	.881	.879	.877
Form 2		.873	.882		.876	.875
Form 3			.877			.878

Note. Alternate form reliabilities are based on Replication 1.

TABLE 5
Test–Retest and Alternate Form Reliability Estimates
for a Two-Stage Multistage Test

	Design 1			Design 2		
	1	2	3	1	2	3
Form 1	.838	.835	.837	.838	.834	.831
Form 2		.842	.842		.837	.829
Form 3			.830			.830

Note. Alternate form reliabilities are based on Replication 1.

test–retest reliabilities were similar for the LFT and three-stage MST designs. Alternate-form and test–retest reliabilities for the two-stage MST designs were somewhat smaller than the other designs. However, this is expected because the two-stage MST design has 20 fewer items than the other designs and thus the examinee ability estimates contain more error of measurement. Finally, within the two- and three-stage designs, no differences were observed between MST Designs 1 and 2.

The correlation evidence presented in Tables 2 through 5 suggests that, for the most part, LFT and the three-stage MST designs provided highly consistent results in terms of ability estimation. Although the two-stage results were not as high as observed with the other designs, the results for all test designs were decidedly similar to those observed with the original test forms. All results were stable across replications within designs, and a high level of consistency was exhibited between the two MST design approaches.

However, for credentialing and licensure testing programs, precision in ability estimation is less important than the accurate classification of examinees into certifiable and noncertifiable groups. Table 6 contains the decision accuracy, false-positive and false-negative rates, and kappas for the first form and replication by test design and 30%, 40%, and 50% pass rates. The decision accuracy was high and exceeded 90% for all pass rates on the real, LFT, and three-stage MST designs. The three-stage MST designs had only slightly higher decision accuracy than the LFT design and lower decision accuracy than the operational form. However, the differences were slight, with misclassifications below 10% and correct classification in excess of 90% for the three-stage MST, LFT, and operational forms at all three pass rates. The two-stage MST results fared only slightly worse, with misclassifications between 10% and 12% and correct classifications exceeding 88% across pass

TABLE 6
Decision Accuracy (DA), False-Positive (FP), and False-Negative (FN)
Rates and Kappas by Test Design and Pass Rate

			3-Stage MST		2-Stage MST	
Pass Rate	Real	LFT	Design 1	Design 2	Design 1	Design 2
30%						
DA	92.2	90.6	91.8	91.9	90.4	89.8
FP	4.6	5.0	4.6	4.3	5.4	5.4
FN	3.2	4.4	3.6	3.8	4.2	4.8
κ	.81	.78	.80	.81	.77	.76
40%						
DA	91.4	90.4	90.8	91.0	89.3	88.9
FP	5.2	5.2	5.0	5.0	5.6	5.9
FN	3.4	4.4	4.2	4.0	5.1	5.2
κ	.82	.80	.81	.81	.78	.77
50%						
DA	90.1	90.4	90.2	90.4	88.3	88.2
FP	5.3	4.9	5.2	5.1	5.5	5.8
FN	4.6	4.7	4.6	4.5	6.2	6.0
κ	.80	.81	.81	.81	.77	.76

Note. Results are based on first form and first replication. MST = multistage test; LFT = linear fixed-length test.

rates. These results are striking, because the two-stage designs are only 40 items in length.

As expected, the false-positive and false-negative rates increased when the passing rate was moved from 30% to 50% because classification errors increases with the proportion of examinees near the passing score. Finally, kappa, a measurement of agreement in classification corrected for chance level agreement, was approximately 0.80 across designs and pass rates, indicating a high level of correct classification. Although not reported, rates for other forms and replications were comparable.

Decision consistency and kappa for Forms 1 and 2 on Replication 1 are reported in Table 7. The percentage of consistently classified examinees was somewhat lower when the two-stage MST was used, regardless of the passing score, compared with the LFT and three-stage MST designs. Similarly, kappa was also substantially lower for the two-stage MST designs than for the LFT and three-stage MST designs. Finally, as expected, consistent classifications decreased as the pass rate increased because more examinees have true abilities near the center of the distribution in this study.

CONCLUSIONS

This study was designed to investigate the merits of several MST designs over LFT designs for a large-volume credentialing exam that requires high levels of decision accuracy and measurement precision throughout the score scale. CAT designs were not considered feasible because the test developers required the ability to re-

TABLE 7
Decision Consistency and Kappa by Test Design and Pass Rate

Pass Rate	Real	LFT	3-Stage MST		2-Stage MST	
			Design 1	Design 2	Design 1	Design 2
30%						
DC	88.5	88.7	87.1	88.7	86.0	84.8
κ	.73	.73	.71	.73	.67	.64
40%						
DC	86.8	86.9	86.4	86.9	84.6	83.3
κ	.73	.73	.72	.73	.68	.65
50%						
DC	86.2	86.4	83.5	86.4	83.4	82.5
κ	.73	.73	.70	.73	.70	.65

Note. Results are based on first and second form, first replication. MST = multistage test; LFT = linear fixed-rate test.

view final test forms before administration. Every effort was made to simulate realistic data for this examination. The item bank was created from four operational administrations. The operational item response theory model was used to calibrate the items for the item bank and to generate the examinee responses. Content specifications were specified as the mean of current operational exams. A realistic distribution of ability scores was chosen, and the passing rates were chosen to span those in recent exam administrations.

The MST designs, too, were realistic in that relatively parsimonious two- and three-stage designs were implemented. Each module was of fixed length, which is a practical consideration and common policy, and the total number of items, as in the operational forms, for the LFT and three-stage MST designs was 60 items. A common finding across test designs was that ability estimates and pass–fail classifications were quite accurate. It is clear that, given the item quality, 60-item exams are sufficient to produce exams with strong psychometric properties. Nevertheless, despite the realism of the simulations, some of the other findings were revealing of challenges faced by credentialing programs and suggest some promising next steps for continued research.

First, the three-stage MST and LFT designs produced results that were comparable to the current operational forms but certainly not better. Higher levels of decision accuracy and consistency, and lower false-positive rates, would be expected if target information functions that exceeded those of the operational forms in the area of the passing score had been able to be specified and met by the automated test assembly software. Figure 5 illustrates this point, because the test information functions from Form 1 of the real, LFT, and each pathway in the 3-Stage MST Design 1 do not vary considerably. Had more aggressive target information functions that could be successfully met been possible, higher decision accuracy and consistency results would have been observed.

Similarly, higher indexes of reliability would be expected for the MST designs if easy and difficult modules that were more dissimilar from the medium-difficulty modules could have been developed. Figure 4 shows that the test assembly software had difficulty consistently meeting the target test information functions even with the relatively modest target test information functions specified in this study for Design 1. Similar results were found in Design 2. Recall that for LFT designs, target information functions were specified as the mean of the operational forms, and for MST designs easy and difficult modules target information functions were translated by only one half a standard deviation. One possible explanation for this finding is that the MST and LFT designs were held to a somewhat higher standard of content matching than the operational exams, and this constraint made it difficult for the test assembly software to closely match the intended target information functions while meeting content specifications. Because only three LFT forms were constructed from a pool derived from four forms, it follows that this difficulty was the result of the variation in the content specification variability of the opera-

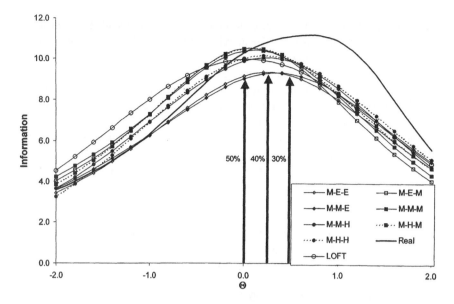

FIGURE 5   Information functions for real, linear fixed-length test, and three-stage multistage test Design 1 (seven possible paths). M = medium; E = easy; H = hard; LOFT = linear on-the-fly test.

tional forms that was not permitted in the automated test assembly procedure. This had the net effect of creating an item bank that simply was not deep enough in items (recall that 75% of the available items were used in item selection) to allow the test assembly software to construct modules that more closely matched the intended target information functions, let alone more aggressively specified target information functions. Had higher levels of adaptation, or more aggressive target information functions that could be successfully met, been possible, then higher classification and measurement precision indexes would have been observed.

Consequently, it is apparent that several of the common challenges in CATs are present in MST designs as well. For example, testing programs are likely going to be required to either develop more test items to enable relatively rigid content, statistical, and overlap (exposure) specifications to be met and/or to create (widen) tolerances in specifications that better enable content, statistical, and security specifications to be appropriately balanced given the resources available and priorities of a testing program. Particularly in the latter approach, additional research and development on the underlying algorithms and user-friendly programs that will readily enable such tolerances to be optimally considered as part of the automated test assembly process would be valuable. Recent applications of combinatorial optimization routines for MST assembly are showing promise in this regard already (e.g., Breithaupt, Ariel, & Veldkamp, 2005). Of course, all automated test assembly programs will require item banks that are both large enough and reflective of the requirements of the test specifications, and so continued research on easily creating additional items through cloning or models in addition to identifying item pool weaknesses is warranted (e.g., van der Linden, Veldkamp, & Reese, 2000; Veldkamp & van der Linden, 2000).

Another finding was that the two variations of the MST designs produced highly comparable results. This was a somewhat surprising finding because it was expected that Design 2 would enable construction of modules that, even in an automated test assembly environment with a restricted item bank, would force the use of highly discriminating items when ability estimates were most accurate. At least two possible explanations exist for this finding. It is possible that an advantage was not seen in this study because a large enough difference was not created between MST Design 1 and Design 2. The difference in allocation of information across three stages of 33%, 33%, and 33% versus 25.0%, 37.5%, and 37.5% was simply not large enough for the effect to materialize in the psychometric quality of the exam. Alternatively, the combination of test length and item bank quality, variability, and size did not enable meaningful differences to be noted with the evaluation criteria used in this study. Nevertheless, it is our belief that the idea of moving the more discriminating items to the later stages is a good one (Chang, Qian, & Ying, 2001). One follow-up study that is planned is to repeat the study using a simulated item bank that better meets the content and statistical specifications of the exam. With a more ideal item bank, the potential advantages of MST and LFT designs can be more precisely determined.

Finally, the psychometric results from the two-stage test designs were only a bit lower (on average, about 2%) than the results from the three-stage MST and LFT designs. Somewhat bigger differences had been expected. Thus, assuming content and validation constraints could be met, a test that is 40 items in length with any of the designs considered in the study might be more than adequate to meet the needs of the credentialing agency. An exam that is two thirds the length could reduce exam costs for candidates and the credentialing agency, reduce testing time, lower item exposure levels, possibly require smaller item banks, and/or might make the current banks better able to meet the needs of the shorter examinations. Of course, this issue of balancing content coverage, measurement precision indicators, and other operational concerns involves careful weighting of the specific needs of the testing agency, characteristics of the examinee population, and the inferences to be drawn from the examination.

ACKNOWLEDGMENTS

This article was completed while the three authors were at the University of Massachusetts, Amherst. An earlier version of this article was presented at the 2002 meeting of the National Council on Measurement in Education, New Orleans, Louisiana.

REFERENCES

Breithaupt, K., Ariel, A., & Veldkamp, B. P. (2005). Automated simultaneous assembly for multi-stage testing. *International Journal of Testing, 5,* 319–330.

Chang, H. H., Qian, J., & Ying, Z. (2001). A-stratified multistage computerized adaptive testing with b blocking. *Applied Psychological Measurement, 25,* 333–341.

Hambleton, R. K., Swaminathan, H., & Rogers, H. J. (1991). *Fundamentals of item response theory.* Newbury Park, CA: Sage.

Jodoin, M. J. (2002). MSTSIM (Version 1.0) [Computer software]. Amherst: University of Massachusetts, Center for Educational Assessment.

Lord, F. M. (1980). *Applications of item response theory to practical testing problems.* Hillsdale, NJ: Lawrence Erlbaum Associates, Inc.

Luecht, R. M. (1996). CASTISEL (Version 1.0) [Computer software]. Philadelphia: National Board of Medical Examiners.

Luecht, R. M., & Nungester, R. (1998). Some practical examples of computer-adaptive sequential testing. *Journal of Educational Measurement, 35,* 239–249.

Mills, C. N., Potenza, M. T., Fremer, J. J., & Ward, W. C. (Eds.). (2002). *Computer-based testing: Building the foundation for future assessments.* Mahwah, NJ: Lawrence Erlbaum Associates, Inc.

Patsula, L. N. (1999). *A comparison of computerized-adaptive testing and multi-stage testing.* Unpublished doctoral dissertation, University of Massachusetts at Amherst.

Patsula, L. N., & Hambleton, R. K. (1999, April). *A comparative study of ability estimates obtained from computer-adaptive and multi-stage testing.* Paper presented at the meeting of the National Council on Measurement in Education, Montreal, Quebec, Canada.

Stocking, M. L., & Lewis, C. (2000). Methods of controlling the exposure of items in CAT. In W. J. van der Linden & C. A. W. Glas (Eds.), *Computerized adaptive testing: Theory and practice* (pp. 163–182). Boston: Kluwer Academic.

van der Linden, W. J., & Glas, C. A. W. (Eds.). (2000). *Computerized adaptive testing: Theory and practice.* Boston: Kluwer Academic.

van der Linden, W. J., Veldkamp, B. P., & Reese, L. M. (2000). An integer programming approach to item pool design. *Applied Psychological Measurement, 24,* 139–150.

Veldkamp, B. P., & van der Linden, W. J. (2000). Designing item pools for computerized adaptive testing. In W. J. van der Linden & C. A. W. Glas (Eds.), *Computerized adaptive testing: Theory and practice* (pp. 149–162). Boston: Kluwer Academic.

Vispoel, W. P. (1998). Reviewing and changing answers on computer-adaptive and self-adaptive vocabulary tests. *Journal of Educational Measurement, 35,* 328–347.

Wainer, H. (with Dorans, N., Eignor, D., Flaugher, R., Green, B., Mislevy, R. J., et al.). (2000). *Computerized adaptive testing: A primer* (2nd ed.). Mahwah, NJ: Lawrence Erlbaum Associates, Inc.

Xing, D. (2000). *Impact of several computer-based testing variables on the psychometric properties of credentialing examinations.* Unpublished doctoral dissertation, University of Massachusetts, Amherst.

Xing, D., & Hambleton, R. K. (2004). Impact of test design, item quality, and item bank size on the psychometric properties of computer-based credentialing examinations. *Educational and Psychological Measurement, 64,* 5–21.

APPLIED MEASUREMENT IN EDUCATION, *19*(3), 221–239

Optimal and Nonoptimal Computer-Based Test Designs for Making Pass–Fail Decisions

Ronald K. Hambleton
Center for Educational Assessment
University of Massachusetts, Amherst

Dehui Xing
British Columbia Ministry of Education
Victoria, British Columbia, Canada

Now that many credentialing exams are being routinely administered by computer, new computer-based test designs, along with item response theory models, are being aggressively researched to identify specific designs that can increase the decision consistency and accuracy of pass–fail decisions. The purpose of this study was to investigate the impact of optimal and nonoptimal multistage test (MST) designs, linear parallel-form test designs (LPFT), and computer adaptive test (CAT) designs on the decision consistency and accuracy of pass–fail decisions. Realistic testing situations matching those of one of the large credentialing agencies were simulated to increase the generalizability of the findings. The conclusions were clear: (a) With the LPFTs, matching test information functions (TIFs) to the mean of the proficiency distribution produced slightly better results than matching them to the passing score; (b) all of the test designs worked better than test construction using random selection of items, subject to content constraints only; (c) CAT performed better than the other test designs; and (d) if matching a TIF to the passing score, the MST design produced a bit better results than the LPFT design. If an argument for the MST design is to be made, it can be made on the basis of slight improvements over the LPFT design and better expected item bank utilization, candidate preference, and the potential for improved diagnostic feedback, compared with the feedback that is possible with fixed linear test forms.

Correspondence should be addressed to Ronald K. Hambleton, Center for Educational Assessment, 152 Hills South, University of Massachusetts, Amherst, MA 01003. E-mail: rkh@educ.umass.edu

Now that many credentialing exams are being routinely administered by computer, new computer-based test designs, along with item response theory models, are being aggressively researched to identify test designs that can increase the decision consistency and accuracy of pass–fail decisions (see, e.g., Luecht & Clauser, 2002; Mills, Potenza, Fremer, & Ward, 2002; van der Linden & Glas, 2000; Wainer, 2000). Computer administration of exams makes it possible to individualize the sequence of exam items or blocks of items to candidates, and item response theory provides the statistical framework to easily and validly link nonparallel forms of exams administered to candidates to a common reporting scale so that a single passing score can be applied to all candidates. Thus, the creativity and technical advances of Frederic Lord in the early 1970s are finally coming to fruition on a large scale at the beginning of the 21st century (Lord, 1970, 1971, 1980). For a full review of the history of adaptive testing, beginning with the work of Binet and Simon in the early 1900s, see Zenisky (2004).

Today, computer-based test designs range from the administration of paper-and-pencil exams at a computer (called *linear parallel-form tests* [LPFTs]) to fully adaptive exams in which item selection depends on the performance of a candidate on previously administered test items (called *computer-adaptive tests* [CATs]) or on groups of items (called *multistage tests* [MSTs]; see, e.g., Lord, 1980; Luecht, 1998b; Luecht & Nungester, 1998; van der Linden & Glas, 2000; Wainer, 2000). Many computer-based test designs for credentialing agencies are available to choose from, and each of these designs has its strengths and weaknesses. For example, a CAT design has the potential to shorten test lengths by 50% for many candidates but requires a large bank of test items (for item security reasons), and that can increase the cost of the testing program. Also, Jodoin, Zenisky, and Hambleton (2002) found increased measurement precision for MSTs compared to LPFTs but found that the item bank that was well suited for constructing the LPFTs was not ideal for building the MSTs of interest. The theoretical advantage of an MST design over an LPFT design was lost when the item bank could not support the construction of MSTs that would meet the often-detailed content and statistical specifications.

Xing and Hambleton (2004) determined that both bank size and item statistical quality were important in enhancing test quality and provided results to show the size of the improvements under conditions that were reasonable in practice. Their study also showed, at least under the conditions and designs simulated, that adaptive test designs (MST and CAT) had no advantage over LPFT (with test information functions [TIFs] centered at the passing score for the exam) on the decision consistency and accuracy of pass–fail decisions. This finding was surprising, given previous research (e.g., Mills, Potenza, Fremer, & Ward, 2002; Wainer, 2000).

One issue that arose from Xing and Hambleton's (2004) research was whether the TIFs used with MSTs and LPFTs should be "matched" to the mean of the candidate proficiency distribution or to the passing score to maximize their effectiveness. When these two points are close, the issue is moot, but when they are different, the better course of action seems less clear. Matching the TIFs to the mean of the candidate proficiency distribution would increase the accuracy of most proficiency estimates, and so decision consistency and accuracy might be expected to be increased. Matching the TIFs to the passing score would ensure higher precision of proficiency scores near the passing score, but precision would be poorer for those candidates somewhat further away from the passing score and could lead to, overall, more misclassifications of candidates. Matching the TIF to the passing score might be especially problematic if the majority of candidates were some distance from the passing score, such as when the pass rate is not close to 50% and proficiency scores are normally distributed.

So, the question becomes "How much difference might it make if a test developer tried to achieve higher measurement precision in the region of the proficiency scale where the bulk of the candidates are located, or to achieve relatively higher measurement precision for candidates in the region of the passing score, when the main purpose of the exam is to make pass–fail decisions?" This is a practical question that arises just about every time a computer-based test is being constructed. What little advice there is in the field (e.g., Hambleton, Swaminathan, & Rogers, 1991) suggests that test information should be maximized at the passing score to enhance the psychometric quality of the exam. At the same time, this is not always practical because of item bank limitations. Also, the answer to the question likely depends on the location of the proficiency distribution in relation to the passing score and the amount of information associated with the TIF at different places along the proficiency continuum. Finally, sometimes credentialing exams have multiple purposes, such as providing failing candidates with detailed diagnostic information as well as making reliable and valid pass–fail decisions, and the same exam, in general, cannot be optimal for achieving both purposes. Learning more about the effect of the positioning of the TIFs in MST and LPFT designs seemed worthy of study.

The purpose of this follow-up to Xing and Hambleton's (2004) study was to investigate the impact of implementing optimal and nonoptimal MST and LPFT designs and CAT designs on the decision consistency and decision accuracy of pass–fail decisions. Realistic situations matching one of the large credentialing agencies were simulated to increase the generalizability of the findings. The primary focus in the study was on MST and LPFT designs, but a CAT design was included also to provide some baseline results.

METHOD

Item Bank

The 600 items in the item bank for the study were selected from an existing credentialing examination. The items were binary scored and calibrated with the three-parameter logistic model using examinee samples in excess of 10,000 (Hambleton et al., 1991; Lord, 1980). Table 1 provides a summary of the item statistics, and Figure 1 provides the information function for the complete bank of

TABLE 1
Candidate and Item Parameter Statistics

Variable	M	SD	Min	Max
Ability Parameters[a]	–0.02	0.99	–3.08	3.33
Item Parameters[b]				
b	0.34	1.32	–1.99	2.50
a	0.71	0.23	0.31	1.10
c	0.20	0.03	0.15	0.25

Note.   Min = minimum; Max = maximum.
[a]$N = 5{,}000$. [b]$n = 600$.

items. The available items were relatively difficult for average proficient candidates (scaled to a mean of 0.0). This is clear from the mean of the item difficulty values (the average b value was 0.34) and the mode of the item bank information function (around $\theta = 1.0$). Rather than work with the specific content categories, for this study the 600 items were randomly assigned to five content categories, and in all test designs implemented, equal numbers of items were selected from each content category. This constraint ensured that the best items statistically could not always be drawn (which would inflate the results over those that might be realistically expected in practice) and paralleled a content constraint that is common.

Item Bank Info

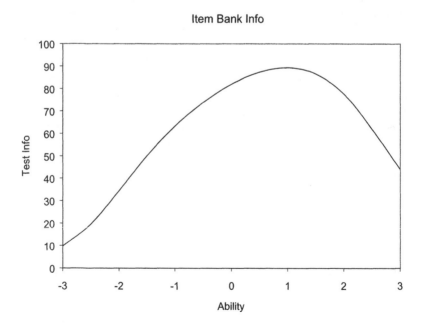

FIGURE 1   Information function for the 600-item bank.

Candidate Population

A sample of 5,000 candidate proficiency scores were drawn from a normal distribution ($M = 0.0$, $SD = 1.0$). The descriptive statistics of the sample appear in Table 1. This sample size was large enough to produce very stable estimates of statistics of interest. Preliminary research suggested that the statistics of interest in this study would vary by less than 0.002 when the sample sizes were as large as 5,000, and thus replication was not necessary.

Passing Scores

The placement of the passing score was chosen as a variable in the study because the placement of the passing score affects pass rates and levels of decision consistency and decision accuracy achieved with any test design. Three choices were made: –0.50, 0.00, and +0.50, corresponding to passing rates of approximately 70%, 50%, and 30%, respectively.

Computer-Based Test Designs

LPFT design. Five nonoverlapping 60-item linear parallel forms from the 600 items were assembled to meet content specifications and target information functions centered at each of the three passing scores on the proficiency continuum: –0.50, 0.00, and +0.50. Maximum exam information was set to a value of approximately 10.0 (a level roughly corresponding to a classical test reliability of .90). Figure 2 shows the five information functions for the LPFTs targeted at 0.00. The five information functions for the LPFTs targeted at either 0.50 or –0.50 are not shown, but they are similar to those in Figure 2, shifted by moving the TIFs to the right by about by 0.50 or to the left by about –0.50, respectively. As these five parallel forms, matched to each passing score, were assigned randomly to candidates (1,000 each), an overall item exposure rate of 0.20 was maintained (five tests, randomly assigned to 5,000 candidates). Of course, lower item exposure levels could have been achieved had more forms been constructed. At the same time, with the use of more items from the bank, the desired targets may have needed to be lower.

MST design. A three-stage test design was used for this study with a routing test and three second-stage modules and three third-stage modules: 20 items in the routing module, 20 items in each second-stage module, and 20 items in each third-stage module. Figure 3 shows the 1-3-3 MST design in place for this study. This design is one of several that have been suggested for the credentialing exam field (see Zenisky, 2004) and has been investigated by the National Board of Medical Examiners (Luecht & Nungester, 1998) and the American Institute of Certified Public Accountants (Luecht, Brumfield, & Breithaupt, 2002). Lord (1980), too,

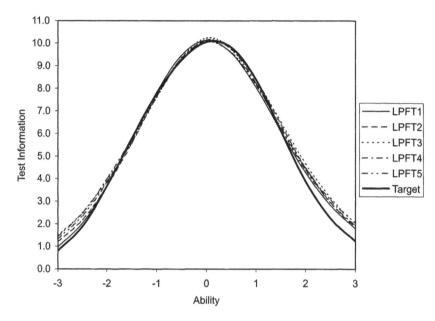

FIGURE 2　Linear parallel form test (LPFT) target and test form information functions ($n = 60$, centered at $\theta = 0.0$).

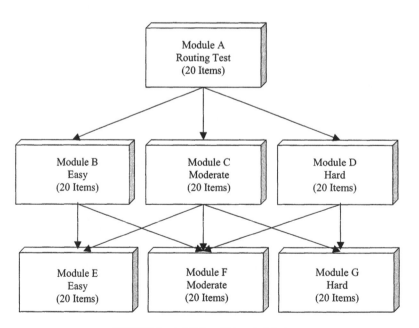

FIGURE 3　A 1-3-3 multistage test design.

suggested that two or three stages and three or four modules at each stage would likely suffice in practice. Item exposure was kept to a level of 0.20. (A few exceptions to this rule are noted later.) The MST design was centered at 0.0 for some simulations and at 0.5 for others.

Lewis and Sheehan (1990), among others, have suggested that when making pass–fail decisions is the sole purpose of a test, multistage designs might be considered when all of the modules are optimal for assessing proficiency in the region of the passing score. The main decision then is one of determining when a sufficient numbers of modules have been administered to achieve a desired level of decision consistency and accuracy. We did not consider the Lewis–Sheehan MST design in this study for two reasons: (a) a concern about producing sufficiently large numbers of test items to provide good measurement precision in the region of the passing score while maintaining the content validity of the exam in any practical applications of the design and (b) our belief that, in the future, credential exam agencies will try to accomplish two purposes in their exam programs—high decision consistency and accuracy, and good diagnostic score reporting to failing candidates—and a design that focuses only on good measurement around the passing score will not be ideal for providing failing candidates with extensive diagnostic information.

MST is an adaptive test design that is attracting attention from credentialing agencies because of several useful features. First, to a limited extent at least, the exam is adapted to candidate performance, which can reduce the amount of exam time and achieve the same or better precision of proficiency estimation. Second, CATs are often criticized because they do not allow candidates to omit items and return to them later or allow candidates to change their answers to items once they have moved on in the exam (Vispoel, Rocklin, & Wang, 1994; Wainer, 1993), whereas within a module within an MST design candidates can omit and return to items and can change their answers prior to moving on the next module. Finally, exam committees can review the way in which test items are grouped together for administration and thereby retain greater control over the exam. This may allow committees, for example, to detect item conflicts or cues (sometimes called *enemies*) and other flaws in item groupings that may go undetected in a CAT design, even with sophisticated test assembly software.

Figure 4 shows the target information functions for a 1-3-3 MST of 60 items centered at 0.0. These MSTs, too, were constructed to have maximum information of about 10.0 (like the LPFTs). The lower 20-item module information functions in Figure 4 correspond to the easy, middle difficulty, and difficult modules. The higher TIFs show the effects of three different routings of candidates:

1. Routing test and then two easy modules (the one on the left)
2. Routing test and then two middle difficulty modules (the one in the middle)
3. Routing test and then two difficult modules (the one on the right).

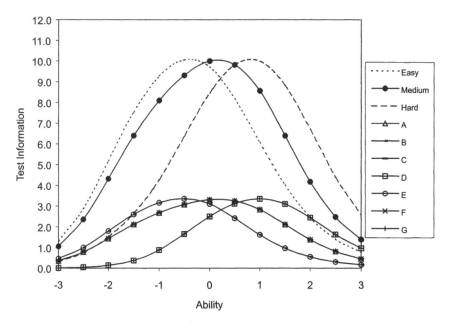

FIGURE 4   Pathway and module target information functions for the three-stage multistage test (1,20,5), (3,20,2), (3,20,2). The test is centered at $\theta = 0.0$. The letters A through G in the legend correspond to the modules shown in Figure 3.

The primary advantage of the MST design over the LPFT design is easily seen: The maximum test information (10) is achieved over a considerably wider range of the proficiency continuum.

A coding scheme was used to distinguish the MST designs. The meaning of, say, a three-stage MST ([1,20,5], [3,20,2], [3,20,2]) is as follows: At the first stage, one module is available with five parallel forms of 20 items; at the second and third stages, three modules are available, each consisting of 20 items, and for each module, two parallel forms are available. In this design, 17 modules would be needed: 9 of middle difficulty, 4 easy, and 4 difficult. Figure 5 shows the seventeen 20-item module information functions that were actually available in the study for the MST centered at a proficiency level of 0.0. These were constructed using the CASTISEL software (Luecht, 1998a). For the purposes of this study, the MST was called *optimal* for the candidates because the mean of the candidate proficiency distribution was 0.0. It would also be optimal for the passing score if the passing score were set to 0.00. It would be called *nonoptimal* for passing scores if they were positioned elsewhere (at –0.50 and +0.50).

Figure 6 shows the seven test information functions associated with the routes possible in a 1-3-3 design using the modules shown in Figure 5. For example, A + B + E was the test information function associated with the routing test and then

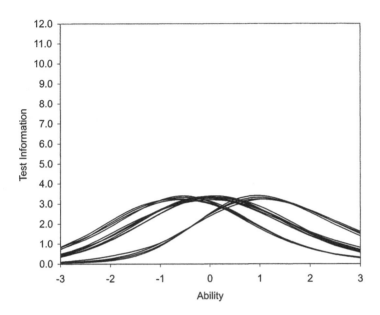

FIGURE 5   Test information functions for all 17 modules of the three-stage multistage test (1,20,5), (3,20,2), (3,20,2). The test is centered at $\theta = 0.0$.

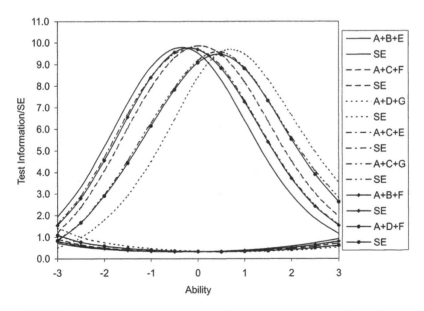

FIGURE 6   Test information and standard error functions for the seven possible multistage test pathways. The test is centered at $\theta = 0.0$. The letter combinations in the legend correspond to the seven possible routes through the MST shown in Figure 3.

229

easy modules at Stages 2 and 3. Routes that might involve transitioning from an easy to a difficult module, or vice versa, after Stage 2, were excluded from the figure but were available to candidates in the application of the MST. (These combinations were very rare in the actual simulations—perhaps they occurred only a couple of times in the total set of simulations.) Figure 6 also shows the standard errors associated with the TIFs.

Two branching strategies were used in the study (for a full review of branching strategies, see Zenisky, 2004). When the MST was centered at 0.0, cut scores were determined on the proficiency scale for assigning approximately equal numbers of candidates to each second-level and third-level module. These were the values –0.50 and +0.50. When the MST was centered at 0.50, the most sensible branching strategy seemed to be one in which candidates with a proficiency estimate near 0.50 would be assigned to the middle-difficulty module. We choose an interval of 0.50 plus or minus approximately 2 standard errors (or $2 \times 0.40 = 0.80$). In this case, for proficiency estimates near 0.50 after Stage 2, the approximate standard error of estimation was .40. This meant that candidates with proficiency estimates between –0.30 and 1.30 after Stage 1 were assigned to the middle-difficulty module. Candidates below –0.30 were assigned to one of the easy modules; candidates above 1.30 were assigned to one of the difficult modules. With a normal distribution of proficiency, the consequence was that, at Stage 2, roughly 43% of the candidates were assigned to one of the easy modules, 45% were assigned to one of the middle-difficulty modules, and 12% were assigned to one of the difficult modules. At Stage 3 the result was that about 40% of the candidates were assigned to one of the easy modules, 50% were assigned to one of the middle-difficulty modules, and 10% were assigned to one of the difficult modules. To retain the 20% item exposure goal with this second assignment strategy, more easy and middle-difficulty modules and fewer hard modules would be needed in practice.

Computerized adaptive test design. A computerized adaptive test with a fixed exam length of 60 items and that met the content specifications was selected for each candidate. The maximum information selection procedure was used subject to the content constraints (see Lord, 1980). Conditional item exposure was held to a value of approximately .30 and an overall item exposure level of .20, same as with the LPFTs and MSTs. In the CAT design implementation, initial candidate proficiency estimates used in selecting the first test item were chosen by a random draw of values uniformly distributed between –1.0 and 0.0 on the proficiency scale. The result was that each candidate began the exam with moderately easy items. The CAT findings in the study provided a baseline for judging results from the other designs.

Proficiency Estimation Algorithm

Expected a posteriori estimation was used to obtain candidate proficiency scores from their item response data (see Bock & Mislevy, 1982). A relatively weak normal prior on proficiency estimation was used to minimize bias: The mean of the prior was set equal to the mean of the candidate population (i.e., 0.0) with a standard deviation twice that of the candidate population (i.e., 2.0).

Exam Length

A fixed exam length of 60 items was chosen for the LPFT, MST, and CAT designs. This allowed the effects of exam design to be studied while controlling for the length of the exam. A few exceptions were introduced, too, to provide some baseline results; however, for reasons of space, these results are excluded from this article.

Item Exposure

With an exam length of 60 items, five nonoverlapping LPFT forms would require 300 items, or 50% of the original bank ($n = 600$), and maintain an item exposure level of 0.20. A overall exposure level of 0.20 and conditional exposure level of 0.30 was maintained with the CAT. With the MSTs, 340 of 600 items (seventeen 20-item modules) were needed (or 57% of the items in the item bank). This potentially placed the MST design at a slight disadvantage because somewhat more items from the bank were needed. However, the target information functions for the MSTs were well within the capability of the item bank and were all met by the exams used in the study (see, e.g., Figure 2, which shows the actual TIFs, centered at 0.0, with the LPFTs).

Evaluation Criteria

In simulation studies, the "true" mastery status of candidates on a credentialing exam can be assumed to be known, and so judging a computer-based test by the extent to which it recovers candidate true mastery status (i.e., known as *decision accuracy* [DA]) was a highly suitable criterion; therefore, it was used in the study. DA is the proportion of decisions resulting from an exam administration to a candidate sample that are in agreement with the true mastery states of candidates. Decision consistency (DC) was another suitable criterion for use in the study and was obtained by simulating each candidate through a test design twice and then determining the consistency of test–retest pass–fail decisions across the sample of candidates.

Data Generation and Compilation of Statistics

Software prepared by Luecht (1998a) was used to construct the five LPFTs and the MSTs centered at each of the passing scores used in the study (–0.50, 0.00, and +0.50). Software prepared by Robin (2000) was used to generate candidate response data, estimate proficiency scores, make candidate pass–fail decisions, and compile the evaluative criteria.

RESULTS

Table 2 provides the DC and DA results for LPFTs centered at 0.00 and 0.50, respectively, with a passing score of –0.50. With this passing score, the pass rate on the exam was 68.6%. The exam with the TIF centered at 0.00 was optimal for estimating proficiency scores (recall that the mean proficiency estimate was 0.00) but not optimal for assessing proficiency scores in the region of the passing score. The exam with the TIF centered at 0.50 was not optimal for estimating proficiency scores and was not optimal either for assessing proficiency scores in the region of the passing score. Five replications were carried out with parallel forms of the exam involving 1,000 candidates each. The exam that was optimal for estimating proficiency provided somewhat better results—about a 1% improvement in both DC (87.4% compared to 86.4%) and DA (91.0% compared to 90.0%). These were the figures obtained by averaging results over the five replications based on 1,000 examinees each.

Table 3 provides the results with a passing score of 0.00 (and a pass rate of about 50.5%). With more candidates near the passing score, somewhat lower DC and DA would be expected for exams of the same quality used when the passing score was set at –0.50. The DC and DA statistics were somewhat lower (about 1%) because of this fact (see the results in Table 2 for a comparison). This time, the TIF centered at 0.0 was optimal for both estimating proficiency scores generally and estimating proficiency scores in the region of the passing score. The results were slightly better (DC and DA levels were up about 0.8% to 0.5%, respectively) than those reported for the exam with the TIF centered at 0.50. This exam was not optimal for estimating proficiency scores generally or proficiency scores in the region of the passing score.

Table 4 provides the results with a passing score of 0.50 (and a corresponding pass rate of 30.8%). This time, the exam with the TIF centered at 0.50 was optimal

TABLE 2
Decision Accuracy (DA) and Decision Consistency(DC),
Linear Parallel-Form Test (5 Forms, Passing Score = –0.50)

	Test Information Centered at 0.0		Test Information Centered at 0.50	
	DC	DA	DC	DA
1	0.869	0.911	0.865	0.899
2	0.876	0.911	0.864	0.896
3	0.874	0.907	0.871	0.901
4	0.879	0.915	0.861	0.904
5	0.874	0.908	0.860	0.902
M	0.874	0.910	0.864	0.900

TABLE 3
Decision Accuracy (DA) and Decision Consistency(DC),
Linear Parallel-Form Test (5 Forms, Passing Score = 0.0)

	Test Information Centered at 0.0		Test Information Centered at 0.50	
	DC	DA	DC	DA
1	0.848	0.894	0.855	0.892
2	0.859	0.899	0.854	0.894
3	0.871	0.906	0.851	0.899
4	0.868	0.897	0.847	0.886
5	0.865	0.899	0.864	0.902
M	0.862	0.899	0.854	0.894

TABLE 4
Decision Accuracy (DA) and Decision Consistency(DC),
Linear Parallel-Form Test (5 forms, Passing Score = 0.50)

	Test Information Centered at 0.0		Test Information Centered at 0.50	
	DC	DA	DC	DA
1	0.874	0.911	0.874	0.910
2	0.876	0.908	0.877	0.911
3	0.868	0.909	0.871	0.900
4	0.879	0.911	0.869	0.904
5	0.884	0.917	0.866	0.911
M	0.876	0.911	0.871	0.907

for estimating proficiency scores near the passing score, but it was not optimal for assessing proficiency scores of candidates generally. The differences in results for the exam constructed to be optimal for the proficiency distribution and the one that was optimal for assessing proficiency near the passing score produced nearly identical results (for DC, 87.6% compared to 87.1%, respectively; for DA, 91.1% compared to 90.7%, respectively). The differences were small with the LPFT design but slightly favored the exam with the TIFs that were matched to the mean of the proficiency distribution.

Tables 5, 6, and 7 provide complete results for the three main test designs (LPFT, MST, and CAT), with optimally and nonoptimally constructed exams (optimal in the sense of matching the mean of the proficiency distribution of candidates and/or the passing score). The baseline results (denoted "BAS" in the tables) obtained by randomly sampling 60 items to create an exam (subject to content constraints only) are also shown. It is clear that all of the test designs showed results that exceeded the exam constructed via random selection of items.

TABLE 5
Decision Accuracy (DA) and Decision Consistency (DC), Linear Parallel-Form Test (LPFT), Multistage Test (MST), and Computer Adaptive Test (CAT; Passing Score = –0.50)

	Test Information Centered at 0.0		Test Information Centered at 0.50	
	DC	DA	DC	DA
LPFT	0.874	0.910	0.864	0.900
MST	0.880	0.912	0.868	0.908
CAT	0.895	0.925		
BAS	0.854	0.891		

Note. BAS = baseline.

TABLE 6
Decision Accuracy (DA) and Decision Consistency (DC), Linear Parallel-Form Test (LPFT), Multistage Test (MST), and Computer Adaptive Test (CAT; Passing Score = 0.0)

	Test Information Centered at 0.0		Test Information Centered at 0.50	
	DC	DA	DC	DA
LPFT	0.862	0.899	0.854	0.894
MST	0.859	0.907	0.849	0.893
CAT	0.871	0.915		
BAS	0.835	0.881		

Note. BAS = baseline.

TABLE 7
Decision Accuracy (DA) and Decision Consistency (DC), Linear Parallel-Form Test (LPFT), Multistage Test (MST), and Computer Adaptive Test (CAT; Passing Score = 0.50)

	Test Information Centered at 0.0		Test Information Centered at 0.50	
	DC	DA	DC	DA
LPFT	0.876	0.911	0.871	0.907
MST	0.873	0.905	0.880	0.916
CAT	0.891	0.927		
BAS	0.862	0.903		

Note. BAS = baseline.

Also, the CAT DC, and DA results were always the highest. These results were expected because with this design each candidate was optimally estimated, and so measurement error and errors in pass–fail classification will correspondingly be minimized. It simply is not possible to obtain a more precise proficiency estimate for any candidate than giving that candidate an optimal set of test items (subject only to the constraints that content specifications and item exposure levels need to be met). Recall, too, that this comparison was made between LPFTs and CATs of 60 items each. If the DC and DA results with the LPFTs were judged as acceptable, these same results could be obtained with a substantially shorter exam length using the CAT design.

Another finding from the study can be seen in Table 5. The exam that was not optimal for measuring candidates or optimal for reducing measurement error in the region of the passing score produced less satisfactory results than the other designs considered in the study (DC = 86.4%, DA = 90.0%). With a passing score of –0.50, proficiency scores centered at 0.00, and the TIF centered at 0.50, the relatively poorest results were obtained (comparing Table 5 and 7 results, excluding the baseline exam; Table 6 results were excluded from the comparison because the passing score was situated in the worst possible place from the perspective of max-imizing DC and DA results). This exam, which produced the poorest results (al-though the differences were small), is displayed in Table 5 and is not uncommon in practice. It could be that, in practice, content specifications are driving exam item selection, and so such an exam might actually be constructed with the TIF shifted to the right of the proficiency distribution and far to the right of the passing score (because it is common to have pass rates in the 80% and above region on many credentialing exams). Were this case to arise in practice, the quality of the exam for the intended purpose of making pass–fail decisions would be somewhat reduced.

Results reported in Table 6 showed the impact of a passing score that is in the middle of the proficiency distribution. All of the psychometric results in Table 6 are a bit lower than the results in either Table 5 or 7. This follows because of the rel-atively large number of candidates near the passing score. Most important, one can see in Table 6 a 1% shift in findings (DC, 85.9% compared to 84.9%; DA, 90.7% compared to 89.3%) that is due to the use of an MST centered at the proficiency distribution and the passing score compared to an MST centered at 0.50. Still, the differences are small.

Table 7 does highlight one important finding in the study: If the TIF of the LPFT or MST design is being matched to the passing score, then the MST produces better results (by 0.9%) than the LPFT. This is an encouraging finding, because the results in Table 7 provide the best indication (of the analyses carried out) of the impact of matching the TIF to the mean of the proficiency distribution or the passing score. The results in Table 6 are difficult to sort out because both the mean of the proficiency dis-tribution and the passing score are at the same place (0.00). The results in Table 5 are less than ideal because neither TIF was matched to the passing score.

TABLE 8
Correlation Between True and Estimated Abilities, Linear Parallel-Form
Test (LPFT), Multistage Test (MST), and Computer Adaptive Test (CAT)

	Test Information Centered at 0.0	Test Information Centered at 0.50
LPFT	0.937	0.930
MST	0.944	0.944
CAT	0.962	
BAS	0.925	

Note. BAS = baseline.

Table 8 provides the correlations obtained between true and estimated proficiency scores with the different test designs and TIFs centered at 0.00 and 0.50. The ordering of the effectiveness of the designs for recovering true proficiency scores was expected: CAT performed best, followed by MST; LPFT; and finally, the baseline exam. The other interesting finding was that the MST design recovered true proficiency scores better than the LPFT design regardless of the placement of the TIF, suggesting the advantage of the MST designs for detailed score reporting, but it is clear that the advantage was small, at least in the analyses carried out in this study.

CONCLUSIONS

The findings reported in the Results section should be important to credentialing agencies, because questions about the merits of various test designs and about the positioning of TIFs in MST and LPFT designs in relation to passing scores are often asked. Should LPFTs and MSTs that are being used to make pass–fail decisions be constructed to optimally measure a group of candidates (with many of the items selected because they maximize information near the middle of the proficiency score distribution) or to optimally function in the region of the passing score? In this study, under what we considered to be some typical conditions, four conclusions can be drawn from the research: (a) With the LPFTs, matching TIFs to the mean of the proficiency distribution produced slightly better results than matching them to the passing score; (b) all of the test designs worked better than test construction using random selection of items; (c) CAT performed better than the other test designs; and (d) if matching a TIF to the passing score, the MST design produced slightly better results than the LPFT design.

The first conclusion was a bit of a surprise, because the findings run counter to the expectations of some researchers. It appears that with the LPFT design, and when the mean of the candidate distribution and the passing score are somewhat apart ($SD = 0.50$ in this study), it may be slightly preferable to center the TIF near the mean of the proficiency distribution. A secondary advantage would be improved measurement precision for many failing candidates that would likely lead to improvements in diagnostic score reporting, something that is now being seriously considered by a number of credentialing agencies.

This finding with the LPFT design may be important for another reason: It highlights the important practical point that exam developers can work with a broader set of item statistics to meet their content specifications. The requirement to build exams that maximize measurement precision near the passing score may not be so very critical in the overall scheme of things and may even be a slight disadvantage from the perspective of maximizing DC and DA in some circumstances.

The second conclusion would of course be expected by psychometricians but may come as a surprise to a number of credentialing agencies that continue to draw items at random from an item bank (sometimes even without considering content specifications). Even a gain of 2% in decision accuracy with 10,000 candidates would affect the mastery status of 200 candidates.

The third conclusion once again highlights the well-known advantages of CAT. However, CAT performed only slightly better than other designs, and this almost certainly is due to the fact that the evaluative criteria were chosen to correspond to a single purpose for the use of credentialing exams, that is, making pass–fail decisions. The CAT design was almost certainly improving the accuracy of proficiency estimation, but these improvements would not all influence the accuracy and consistency of decision making.

The fourth conclusion may be the most interesting and useful: With the TIF matched to the passing score, the MST design produced slightly better results than the LPFT design. This would mean, for example, that were an MST design in place, test developers could better use their item banks because they allow for a wider spread of item difficulties, and meeting content specifications may be a bit easier to do. Some researchers might note that the LPFT design produced statistical results nearly equivalent to the MST design and would be easier to implement in practice. The possible danger in practice that was not seen in this simulation study, because of the design, is the shortcomings of an item bank for constructing lots of exams functioning near the passing score (see, e.g., Jodoin et al., 2002). Also, with the construction of fewer exams because of the specifications, item exposure levels would increase with the risk of a drop in exam validity. But relaxing or lowering the test specifications to permit more exams to be generated may not be the answer either because TIFs would drop, and so would the levels of DC and DA. An MST would seem to have more potential for fully using an item bank and reducing the problems that are likely to result with the LPFT design.

If there is a substantial effect on DC and DA due to test designs such as CAT and MST, which individualize the testing, it will be found only with simulations more extreme and varied than those carried out in this study. We note, too, that Jodoin et al. (2002), Zenisky (2004), and Xing and Hambleton (2004) were not able to show very much difference among the test designs they studied. One study we would like to see carried out is one with the second- and third-stage modules set up to be much further apart than they were in this study. This revised MST design might highlight the advantages of individualizing the testing. Still, the CAT results are really not much better, and at best all an MST design could do is equal the CAT design results. A second study may be worthwhile, too. Changes in TIF from, say, 8 to 10, which were typical in this study, were having only a small impact on standard errors of proficiency estimation (.354–.316). The only way substantial gains due to test design or item selection will be seen in practice is if changes in TIF are quite substantial and strategically placed (e.g., substantial changes in the TIF around the mean of the proficiency distribution would be consequential if the passing score were not too far away). Perhaps more research along these general lines would be helpful.

ACKNOWLEDGMENT

Support for this research was provided by a contract from the American Institute for Certified Public Accountants to the University of Massachusetts, Amherst, Center for Educational Assessment, Stephen G. Sireci, principal investigator.

REFERENCES

Bock, B. D., & Mislevy, R. J. (1982). Adaptive EAP estimation of ability in a microcomputer environment. *Applied Psychological Measurement, 6,* 431–444.

Hambleton, R. K., Swaminathan, H., & Rogers, H. J. (1991). *Fundamentals of item response theory.* Newbury Park, CA: Sage.

Jodoin, M., Zenisky, A., & Hambleton, R. K. (2002, April). *Comparison of the psychometric properties of several computer-based test designs for credentialing exams.* Paper presented at the meeting of the National Council on Measurement in Education, New Orleans, LA.

Lewis, C., & Sheehan, K. (1990). Using Bayesian decision theory to design a computerized mastery test. *Applied Psychological Measurement, 29,* 129–146.

Lord, F. M. (1970). Some test theory for tailored testing. In W. H. Holtzman (Ed.), *Computer-assisted instruction, testing, and guidance* (pp. 139–183). New York: Harper & Row.

Lord, F. M. (1971). A theoretical study of two-stage testing. *Psychometrika, 36,* 227–242.

Lord, F. M. (1980). *Applications of item response theory to practical testing problems.* Hillsdale, NJ: Lawrence Erlbaum Associates, Inc.

Luecht, R. M. (1998a). CASTISEL [Computer software]. Philadelphia: National Board of Medical Examiners.

Luecht, R. M. (1998b). Computer-assisted test assembly using optimization heuristics. *Applied Psychological Measurement, 22,* 224–236.

Luecht, R. M., Brumfield, T., & Breithaupt, K. (2002, April). *A testlet-assembly design for the Uniform CPA Exam.* Paper presented at the meeting of the National Council on Measurement in Education, New Orleans, LA.

Luecht, R. M., & Clauser, B. E. (2002). Test models for complex computer-based testing. In C. N. Mills, M. T. Potenza, J. J. Fremer, & W. C. Ward (Eds.), *Computer-based testing: Building the foundation for future assessments* (pp. 67–88). Mahwah, NJ: Lawrence Erlbaum Associates, Inc.

Luecht, R. M., & Nungester, R. (1998). Some practical examples of computer-adaptive sequential testing. *Journal of Educational Measurement, 35,* 229–249.

Mills, C. N., Potenza, M. T., Fremer, J. J., & Ward, W. C. (Eds.). (2002). *Computer-based testing: Building the foundation for future assessments.* Mahwah, NJ: Lawrence Erlbaum Associates, Inc.

Robin, F. (2000). CBTS: Computer-based testing simulation and analysis [Computer software]. Amherst: University of Massachusetts, Center for Educational Assessment.

van der Linden, W. J., & Glas, C. A. W. (Eds.). (2000). *Computer adaptive testing: Theory and practice.* Boston: Kluwer Academic.

Vispoel, W. P., Rocklin, T. R., & Wang, T. (1994). Individual differences and test administration procedures: A comparison of fixed-item, computer-adaptive, and self-adaptive testing. *Applied Measurement in Education, 7,* 53–79.

Wainer, H. (1993). Some practical considerations when converting a linearly administered test to an adaptive format. *Educational Measurement: Issues and Practice, 12*(1), 15–20.

Wainer, H. (Ed.). (2000). *Computerized adaptive testing: A primer* (2nd ed.). Mahwah, NJ: Lawrence Erlbaum Associates, Inc.

Xing, D., & Hambleton, R. K. (2004). Impact of test design, item quality, and item bank size on the psychometric properties of computer-based credentialing examinations. *Educational and Psychological Measurement, 64,* 5–21.

Zenisky, A. L. (2004). *Evaluating the effects of several multi-stage testing design variables on selected psychometric outcomes for certification and licensure assessment.* Unpublished doctoral thesis, University of Massachusetts, Amherst.

APPLIED MEASUREMENT IN EDUCATION, *19*(3), 241–255

How Big Is Big Enough?
Sample Size Requirements for CAST
Item Parameter Estimation

Siang Chee Chuah and Fritz Drasgow
Department of Psychology
University of Illinois at Urbana-Champaign

Richard Luecht
Department of Educational Research Methodology
University of North Carolina at Greensboro

Adaptive tests offer the advantages of reduced test length and increased accuracy in ability estimation. However, adaptive tests require large pools of precalibrated items. This study looks at the development of an item pool for 1 type of adaptive administration: the computer-adaptive sequential test. An important issue is the sample size required for adequate estimation of item response theory item parameters. The authors simulated responses of 300, 500, and 1,000 respondents per item, estimated item parameters with the BILOG program, and then evaluated the adequacy of the parameter estimates. The results suggest that sample sizes as small as 300 respondents per item are adequate for estimating ability and classifying examinees as masters or nonmasters.

In this article, we examine some practical issues concerning the development of an item pool for a computer adaptive test. The test administration procedure examined here, the *computer-adaptive sequential test* (CAST; Luecht, 2000; Luecht & Nungester, 1998, 2000), is a compromise between fully adaptive and conventional tests: CAST provides a general framework for designing and building multistage adaptive tests that use preconstructed multi-item modules or *testlets*. For this study, we used a 1-3-3 CAST design. Under this design, all examinees are administered an initial test module in Stage 1, denoted *1M* in Figure 1. On the basis of their performance on 1M, examinees are routed to an easy (Module 2E in Figure 1), moderately difficult (2M), or hard (2H) module in Stage 2 of the CAST. Ex-

Correspondence should be addressed to Siang Chee Chuah, American Institute for Certified Public Accountants, 1230 Parkway Ave., Suite 311, Ewing, NJ 08628. E-mail: dchuah@aicpa.org

Stage #1 ⇨ *Stage #2* ⇨ *Stage #3*

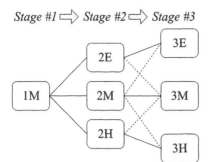

FIGURE 1   CAST panel configuration for the simulation study. M = moderately difficult; E = easy; H = hard.

aminees are allowed to branch up or down only one level as they go to the third CAST stage (Luecht & Nungester, 2000). Thus, an examinee who does well on 2E would be branched to 3M, but not to 3H, and an examinee who does poorly on 2H would be administered 3M.

The set of seven modules in Figure 1 is referred to as a *CAST panel*. To prevent compromise in a continuous testing program, automated test assembly (ATA) procedures can be used to create hundreds of panels from a large item pool. Several panels can be available on any given day of testing, and different sets of panels can be downloaded to test administration sites daily.

Of course, a CAST panel will not provide the measurement precision of a fully adaptive test because the unit of adaptation is larger. But adaptive tests that use content-balancing heuristics to meet detailed content specifications are likewise not fully adaptive. Instead, numerous constraints may be placed on the item selection algorithm so that the content specifications are satisfied. Stocking and Swanson (1993), for example, devised a method for imposing many constraints simultaneously. Martha Stocking (personal communication, June 16, 1995) has described computerized adaptive tests (CATs) with numerous constraints as "BATs" (barely adaptive tests).

An important virtue of CAST is that test developers can manually inspect each panel before it is administered operationally. Consequently, problems discernable only to content experts can be identified and corrected (and, possibly, additional constraints can subsequently be specified for the ATA). A fully adaptive CAT or a shadow test CAT (van der Linden, 2000), on the other hand, is created on the fly; test developers are not able to inspect the set of items before test administration to ensure that the test is satisfactory. Thus, test developers cannot be absolutely certain that a CAT meets the high standards of a carefully assembled conventional test.

SAMPLE SIZE REQUIREMENTS

For ATA procedures to be used to assemble hundreds of CAST panels, a large pool of precalibrated items must be available. A testing program may use its own item writers or contract with a vendor to write many thousands of new items. A practical issue of critical importance involves determining how to pretest the new items so that item response theory (IRT) item parameters can be estimated. Estimated item parameters are needed for at least two tasks: (a) assembling CAST panels via ATA and (b) estimating ability after an examinee completes the test.

There are numerous strategies for pretesting new items. Perhaps most common is embedding a few new items or even an entire experimental section on an operational test. Although few, if any, testing programs use the experimental pretest items in actual scoring, examinees are seldom made aware of which items are experimental. The rationale is simple: In a high-stakes testing program, examinees should be motivated to do well on all the items when they do not know which items are operational versus experimental. This approach to pretesting helps to ensure that very high quality data are available for estimating the item parameters needed to build new test forms. Unfortunately, when a testing program transitions from paper-and-pencil testing on a few days per year to computerized testing on a continuous basis, thousands of items need to be calibrated, and seeding a handful of new items into the last few paper-and-pencil test forms many not be sufficient.

Alternatively, testing programs can seek volunteers or pay people to take sets of new items. Suppose a testing program pays examinees $25 to answer 100 items. If data from 1,000 examinees are needed to estimate IRT item parameters for each item, and the testing program needs to calibrate 5,000 new items, then the total payment to examinees would be $1,250,000 (5,000 items × 1,000 examinees per item/100 items per examinee × $25).

Dedicated pretesting is clearly a high-cost enterprise, with sample size driving the degree of cost. Furthermore, comparability of the pretest samples to the real examination population in terms of ability and motivation remains questionable, despite the money spent. In addition, there are expenses associated with recruiting and scheduling 50,000 examinees, administering the items, room rental for the test administration, and numerous other incidentals. Obviously, the cost is high and the logistics of scheduling this many examinees would be very difficult.

Thus, it is very important to address the question of the minimum sample size for a calibration sample that is adequate for estimating item parameters. Obviously, if 500 examinees per item were sufficient, costs would be substantially reduced.

PREVIOUS RESEARCH

There is a body of research that has examined the minimum sample size requirements for item parameter estimation. In 1968, Lord suggested that samples larger than 1,000 respondents, responding to at least 50 items, were necessary for adequate item parameter estimation for the three-parameter logistic model. Lord (1968) used joint maximum likelihood estimation in which ability parameters and item parameters were estimated simultaneously. For this estimation method, simulations have shown little increase in estimation accuracy for samples of more than 1,000 respondents (Hulin, Lissak, & Drasgow, 1982).

Goldman and Raju (1986) examined the accuracy of person parameter estimates for the one- and two-parameter logistic model. They based their study on item parameters estimated from an attitude survey. Samples of 250, 500, and 1,000 simulated respondents were generated, and the LOGIST computer program (Wood & Lord, 1976; Wood, Wingersky, & Lord, 1976) was used to simultaneously estimate item and person parameters. Estimation precision was evaluated by correlating estimated abilities with the simulation ability parameters. Correlations between the estimated and true person parameters, using the two-parameter logistic model, ranged from .964 to 1.000. Goldman and Raju concluded that sample sizes of 250 respondents were sufficient to estimate item parameters that could in turn be used to estimate ability parameters.

Since Lord's seminal article in 1968, there have been improvements in item parameter estimation. Swaminathan and Gifford (1986) advocated a joint Bayesian estimation procedure for the three-parameter logistic model. They showed that their Bayesian procedure outperformed joint maximum likelihood estimation across sample sizes of 100, 200, and 400 simulated respondents on tests with 25 and 35 items.

Perhaps the most important theoretical advance was Bock and Lieberman's (1970) introduction of marginal maximum likelihood estimation (MMLE); here, ability parameters are removed from the likelihood equation by integrating with respect to an ability density. Bock and Aitkin (1981) used the expectation-maximization algorithm to develop an efficient estimation procedure for MMLE that is the basis for the BILOG (Mislevy & Bock, 1990) computer program. The BILOG program also allows prior distributions to be assumed for each item parameter, thus allowing marginal Bayesian estimation.

Harwell and Janosky (1991) examined the minimum sample size requirements for the Bayesian procedure implemented in BILOG. The two-parameter logistic model was used to simulate samples ranging in size from 75 to 1,000 response patterns for tests with 15 and 25 items. They concluded that samples of 250 respondents and tests with as few as 15 items were sufficient for the Bayesian estimation approach to the two-parameter logistic model. This conclusion agrees with the findings of Drasgow (1989) for the two-parameter logistic model; he used MMLE and found item parameters to be generally well estimated for samples as small as 200.

SAMPLE SIZE REQUIREMENTS FOR CAST

To answer the question "What is an adequate sample size for item parameter estimation for CAST?," we conducted simulations contrasting an ideal baseline case,

TABLE 1
Classification Outcomes

	True Status	
Test Decision	Master: $\theta \geq \theta_o$	Nonmaster: $\theta < \theta_o$
Pass: $\hat{\theta} \geq \theta_o$	Correct	False-positive
Fail: $\hat{\theta} < \theta_o$	False-negative	Correct

where there was no error in the item parameters, to cases of different calibration sample sizes. Sample size for item calibration was considered adequate to the extent that there was little decrement in measurement accuracy from the baseline condition (where panels were assembled with true simulation item parameters and ability was estimated with true simulation item parameters) to the comparison conditions (where panels were assembled using estimated item parameters and ability was estimated with estimated item parameters).

Baseline information was established by assembling CAST panels using true item parameters (i.e., the item parameters used in the simulation), simulating a large number of CAST test administrations, and estimating ability using the true simulation item parameters.

To examine the effects of item parameter estimation error, we repeated the above baseline procedure with additional steps needed to estimate item parameters. We first simulated a pretest sample and estimated item parameters. We then used the estimated item parameters to assemble CAST panels, simulated a large number of CAST test administrations, and estimated ability using the estimated item parameters.

Two outcome measures were considered. First, we computed the correlation of estimated ability with true ability for the baseline and comparison conditions. The second outcome considered is relevant in the context of licensing and credentialing exams. Given a cut score θ_o that differentiates between passing and failing, what percentage of examinees are correctly classified? Table 1 shows the four possible outcomes when θ and $\hat{\theta}$ are compared to the cut score. Again, the upper bound on classification accuracy is obtained in the baseline condition when simulation item parameters are used to assemble CAST panels and estimate ability.

METHOD

Simulation Parameters

The simulation data were based on item parameters estimated from samples of examinees completing conventional paper-and-pencil administrations of the Uniform Certified Public Accountant Examination (UCPAE). The current version of the UCPAE has four subtests: (a) Audit, (b) Financial Accounting and Reporting, (c) Accounting and Reporting, and (d) Legal and Professional Responsibilities. Data from the Audit test were used in this study.

Item parameters for 450 items were available for analysis. BILOG (Mislevy & Bock, 1990) was used to fit the three-parameter logistic model,

$$P_i(\theta) = c_i + \frac{1 - c_i}{1 + e^{-1.7a_i(\theta - b_i)}} \tag{1}$$

to the data from the Audit test using default settings, except that 30 quadrature points were specified. Responses from more than 20,000 candidates were available for each item, and consequently item parameters were estimated very accurately. These item parameters estimates are henceforth denoted as the *true item parameters*. One caveat about the item parameters is the fact that many of the items have information functions that peak around the passing cut score of the test. This is not surprising because well-developed certification item pools should have their items focused around the passing cut score in order to maximize categorization accuracy in a certification test.

Throughout the remainder of this study, item responses were generated using the item parameters described earlier. In addition, each simulated respondent's ability level was randomly sampled from a standard normal distribution $N(0, 1)$. Item responses were generated by first computing the probability of correctly answering items by Equation 1 and then sampling uniform random numbers from the interval $(0, 1)$. If the uniform random number was equal to or less than the probability of correctly answering item i, then item i was scored as correct. Otherwise, item i was scored as incorrect.

Pretest Sample Simulation Procedure

It is not realistic to expect examinees to answer every item in a large item pool. The number of items would overwhelm even the most determined examinee. Therefore, we assumed that each examinee would answer 50 items. To simulate the sparse matrix of responses to items in the item pool, we used the design matrix shown in Table 2. The first 50 items served as anchor items (i.e., items that participants have in common) and were administered to the first group of simulated respondents. These 50 items were chosen at random from the item pool because in a real testing situation we would not be able to anticipate the quality of the item parameters before pretesting. Each subsequent group was administered 5 items from the set of 50 anchor items and 45 unique items. These 5-item linking blocks were rotated because we expect that testing programs would want to control for over-

TABLE 2

Design Matrix for Items Administered to Pretest Sample Used for Item Parameter Estimation

Item No.	1–5	6–10	11–15	16–20	21–25	26–30	31–35	36–40	41–45	46–50	51–95	96–140	141–185	186–230	231–275	276–320	321–365	366–410	411–455	Total Items Taken
n	5	5	5	5	5	5	5	5	5	5	45	45	45	45	45	45	45	45	45	
	X	X	X	X	X	X	X	X	X	X										50
	X										X									50
		X										X								50
			X										X							50
				X										X						50
					X										X					50
						X										X				50
							X										X			50
								X										X		50
									X										X	50

exposure of anchor items. If the same anchor items were administered to every examinee in a real testing situation, it is likely that the anchor items would risk being compromised. The use of 5 items as the linking block was a compromise between maximizing the number of new pretest items and adequately linking the sets of unique items to the common metric. Additional research to determine the optimal number of linking items would be most informative. However, this issue is beyond the scope of this study.

Pretest data sets were created by simulating a fixed number of examinees answering each item. Specifically, we assumed that pretest procedures would be designed so that 300, 500, or 1,000 examinees would answer Items 51 to 450. Because of the linking procedure, the number of responses simulated for Items 1 to 50 was twice as large as for Items 51 to 450.

Item parameters were then estimated using BILOG (Mislevy & Bock, 1990). The default settings were used to estimate item parameters. MMLE was used to estimate the difficulty parameter, and marginal maximum a posteriori was used to estimate the discrimination and lower asymptote parameters. Item parameter estimation converged without excessive iterations, which suggests that the linking blocks of five items were adequate.

CAST Modules

The ATA process used for these simulations employed a program called CASTISEL (Luecht, 1998a). CASTISEL implements the normalized weighted absolute deviation heuristic (Luecht, 1998b) to build multistage tests with multiple objective functions (test information targets) and associated test-level content specifications. The software uses a partitioning algorithm (Luecht, 1998a) to optimally allocate the test-level content to the various CAST stages. This same software has been extensively used in other multistage adaptive testing research and even operationally by several testing programs.

Four sets of 450 item parameters were submitted to CASTISEL to build CAST panels. The four sets of item parameters were (a) the true simulation item parameters (i.e., the item parameters estimated from the large samples of Audit examinees), (b) the item parameters estimated from 300 simulees per item, (c) the item parameters estimated from 500 simulees per item, and (d) the item parameters estimated from 1,000 simulees per item. Two nonoverlapping CAST panels were assembled from each set of item parameters. The 1-3-3 CAST panel design shown in Figure 1 was used with 20 items per module, so that each panel consisted of 140 items.

We assumed that examinees would be routed through the CAST on the basis of the number of items per module that they answered correctly (i.e., number-right scoring with no correction for guessing). The reason for the use of number-right scoring, rather than an IRT procedure in the routing procedure, is because of limitations of the actual test deployment drivers to be used in the operational UCPAE test. We also assumed that the testing program would want approximately equal numbers of examinees to take each module in Stages 2 and 3. Therefore, simulations were run to determine cut scores for the number-right score that would distribute the respondents equally (i.e., approximately one third of the respondents would take each module in Stages 2 and 3). This approach enabled equal exposure of each module, thereby minimizing overexposure of items from any particular test module.

In sum, eight CAST panels were created (two panels from the true simulation item parameters and two panels from each of the three sets of estimated item parameters). We then simulated response patterns for 5,000 respondents for each of the eight panels. As before, the simulated respondent's ability level was randomly sampled from a standard normal distribution $N(0, 1)$.

It is important to note that the "true" simulation item parameters were always used to generate responses. Thus, the item parameters used to simulate data matched the item parameters used to assemble panels and estimate ability for two CAST panels (the ones created from the simulation parameters). However, to simulate estimation error, the estimated item parameters were used to assemble panels and estimate the simulees' abilities for the remaining six panels.

As the final step in the CAST administration procedure, each simulee's ability was estimated by maximum likelihood to obtain the $\hat{\theta}$ values used for subsequent analysis. These ability estimates were used to determine the classification accuracy of pass–decisions and correlated with the θ values used to generate responses.

RESULTS

Item Information

To examine the comparability of the CAST panels for the different sets of item parameter estimates, we computed information functions for each of the seven modules in the 1-3-3 design. Figure 2 shows the module information functions of the first CAST panel constructed from the simulation item parameters, as well as module information functions for CAST panels assembled from estimated item parameters (plots of module information functions for the other CAST panels were very similar). For the panels assembled from estimated item parameters, we computed both the true information functions (i.e., the information functions computed using the true simulation item parameters) and the estimated information functions (i.e., the information functions computed using estimated item parameters).

Note that the information function for the Stage 1 module never exceeds 12 when the correct values of the item parameters are used in its calculation. When estimated item parameters are used, the function reaches 14 in the $N = 1,000$ sample

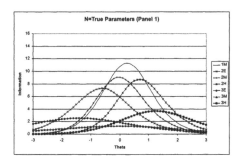
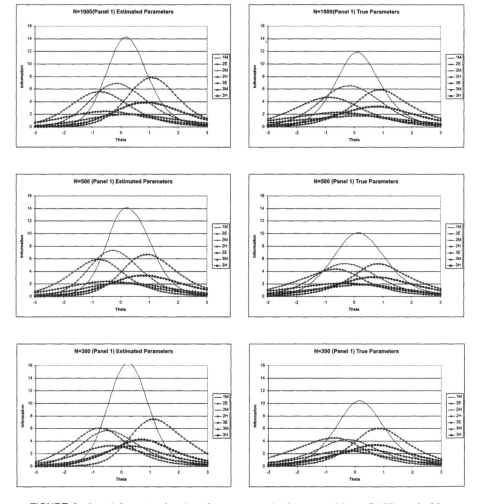

FIGURE 2   Item information functions for computer-adaptive sequential test CAST panels. M = moderately difficult; E = easy; H = hard.

and exceeds 16 for $N = 300$. The inflation in information function values occurs because of estimation errors in discrimination parameters; the a_i parameters of some items are overestimated, and the ATA algorithm is designed to select items with large a_i parameters (i.e., to match highly informative targets within particular regions of the score scale). In some sense, this finding is specific to the way that the CASTISEL software was designed; that is, the Stage 1 module is chosen first and tends to acquire as much of the test-level information as possible; this same pattern would be exhibited by any adaptive test that uses a maximum-information criterion for item selection. Figure 2 shows that, as expected, the size of the discrepancy is inversely related to the sample size used to estimate item parameters. These results suggest that the use of small sample sizes for pretesting items may lead to unrealistically optimistic beliefs about the precision of ability estimates. Reducing the amount of test information targeted for the Stage 1 modules when item parameters have been estimated in small samples errors might ameliorate this problem.

Figure 2 also shows that CASTISEL was somewhat less effective when item parameters have been estimated in small samples. The information function for the Stage 1 module nearly reaches 12 for the simulation item parameters and the $N = 1,000$ estimation sample but is only about 10 for the $N = 500$ and $N = 300$ estimation samples. The Stage 2 hard module (2H) information function exceeds 8 when it was assembled using the simulation item parameters but reaches only 6 when assembly is based on estimated item parameters. Similar trends are apparent for the other two Stage 2 modules (2E and 2M). Finally, the Stage 3 hard module (3H) information function reaches a slightly higher maximum when simulation parameters were used for assembly than when estimated parameters were used. Again, the same trend is seen for the other Stage 3 modules.

Accuracy of Ability Estimates

Table 3 shows the correlations between ability estimates ($\hat{\theta}$ values) and the simulation abilities (θ values). Correlations are provided for ability estimates computed with item parameters estimated from samples of $N = 300$, 500, and 1,000, as well as computed from the simulation item parameters. There is little difference among

TABLE 3
Correlations of the Simulation Ability Parameters
With Estimated Ability Parameters

N	Panel 1	Panel 2	Average
True	.964	.967	.965
1,000	.957	.953	.955
500	.955	.957	.956
300	.955	.948	.952

the correlations shown in Table 3. Thus, using estimated item parameters, even estimated from as few as 300 responses per item, seems to have little effect on ability estimation.

Accuracy of Classification

For licensing and credentialing exams, the correlation of true and estimated ability is of secondary importance; the major issue is the rate of correctly classifying candidates as masters versus nonmasters. These classification rates are presented in Table 4 for the CAST panels studied in this article. Using parameters estimated from $N = 300$ responses per item to assemble panels and estimate ability, we were able to accurately classify 93.57% of the simulated respondents; the correct classification rate was 94.07% when the simulation parameters were used for ATA and ability estimation. Paralleling the results of our correlational analyses, using estimated item parameters in place of the simulation item parameters has little apparent effect on classification accuracy, even when as few as 300 responses per item are available.

From a mastery test perspective, it is important not only to assess the overall classification accuracy of the test but also to look at how inaccurate classifications occur: the proportions of false negatives and false positives. Table 1 illustrates how these errors can occur. Percentages of false negatives—candidates who are truly masters but who fail the test—are given in Table 4. There is a trend to make more false-negative errors (3.52%) when using parameters estimated from $N = 300$ responses per item than when using the true item parameters (2.87%). On the other hand, using the $N = 300$ item parameter estimates

TABLE 4
Percentages of Correct Classifications and Bias Estimates

N	Panel 1 %	Panel 2 %	Average %
300			
Correct classification	93.74	93.40	93.57
False negative	3.60	3.44	3.52
500			
Correct classification	92.94	93.46	93.20
False negative	4.52	3.72	4.12
1,000			
Correct classification	93.92	93.54	93.73
False negative	3.20	3.38	3.29
True			
Correct classification	93.62	94.52	94.07
False negative	2.98	2.76	2.87

produces a lower false-positive rate (2.91%) than using the true simulation parameters (3.06%).

DISCUSSION

Both the correlational analysis and the classification accuracy results support the conclusion that pretesting items with just 300 examinees is adequate when one's goal is to estimate item parameters for ability estimation. It is important, however, to note several caveats to this conclusion. First, although ability estimates were satisfactory, other results derived from item parameters estimated in such a small sample were less satisfactory. For example, item and test information functions computed from the $N = 300$ condition were of limited accuracy. The discrimination parameters of some items were overestimated, and so the apparent quality of these items provides a false impression of the extent to which they contribute to measurement accuracy. Thus, collecting data from 300 examinees per item is adequate for ability estimation but is clearly inadequate for other purposes. Inflated discrimination parameters can be a problem in Bayesian estimation, particularly with small pretest samples, when the mean of the prior for item discrimination is set at a relatively high value. This problem is exacerbated by the ATA software because it selects items with higher discrimination parameters in order to maximize test information.

A second caveat is more subtle: All of our simulees were fully motivated; that is, we simulated responses according to the three-parameter logistic model with abilities sampled from the standard normal distribution. In practice, paying examinees $25 to spend several hours answering test items may not motivate everyone to do their best. Some examinees may lose interest and their effort level may dwindle; others may simply provide answers without reading the questions. Thus, our conclusion can be stated more carefully as "Item parameters can be estimated from the responses of 300 highly motivated examinees per item."

What proportion of actual pretest examinees is highly motivated? Analyses based on appropriateness measurement (Levine & Rubin, 1979), also termed *person-fit* (Meijer & Sijtsma, 2001), might be used to identify poorly motivated examinees and remove them from the sample. In this way, we could determine the proportion of motivated versus unmotivated examinees and better understand how many examinees must be tested in order to obtain 300 motivated examinees per item. Alternatively, Rost's (1990) mixture model might be fitted to the pretest data to estimate directly the proportion of poorly motivated examinees. Research on the pervasiveness of unmotivated research participants is needed to better answer the question of how large a sample size is needed for pretesting new items.

Another caveat is that the simulees in the pretest samples had ability parameters drawn from the same distribution as those we simulated completing the CAST.

Even if test developers go to some lengths to obtain a pretest sample that is similar to their examinee population, it is unlikely that the match will be perfect. Of course, IRT item parameters are subpopulation invariant, but the quality of estimates of parameters is always affected by the sample from which they are computed. The consequences of any mismatch between the pretest sample and the actual examinee population are unknown and constitute another area for further research.

Other areas for future work relate to improved ATA strategies and software that can be used to implement CAST (also see Luecht, 2000; Luecht, Brumfield, & Breithaupt, 2002). For this study, we were dependent on CASTISEL, which was developed strictly as a research software tool to demonstrate particular types of multistage adaptive testing designs (Luecht & Nungester, 1998). Despite its rather extensive research and operational use to date, the software remains limited with respect to offering certain desirable ATA strategies and options (e.g., allowing controlled item reuse across all modules and replications, providing less emphasis on the stages as a means of ordering the item selections within each panel). Unfortunately, ATA alternatives to CASTISEL are not yet available. Nonetheless, CASTISEL appears to have worked reasonably well for us. Moreover, although module information functions were somewhat affected by estimation error in item parameters, the overall effect on ability estimates was inconsequential. Other ATA strategies may be less affected by estimation error (but, of course, they may be more affected as well).

In sum, pretesting items with relatively small samples appears satisfactory for launching a CAST-based continuous testing program that requires a large item pool. As operational data are collected, item parameters should be reestimated. Although better estimated item parameters seem unlikely to improve the quality of ability estimation, they would give test developers a better understanding of the precision of measurement (e.g., the conditional standard error of $\hat{\theta}$) and be useful in other analyses, such as differential item functioning.

ACKNOWLEDGMENT

Siang Chee Chuah is now at the American Institute for Certified Public Accountants in Ewing, New Jersey.

REFERENCES

Bock, R. D., & Aitkin, M. (1981). Marginal maximum likelihood estimation of item parameters: An application of an EM algorithm. *Psychometrika, 46,* 443–459.

Bock, R. D., & Lieberman, M. (1970). Fitting a response model for N dichotomously scored items. *Psychometrika, 35,* 179–197.

Drasgow, F. (1989). An evaluation of marginal maximum likelihood estimation for the two-parameter logistic model. *Applied Psychological Measurement, 13,* 77–90.

Goldman, S. H., & Raju, N. S. (1986). Recovery of one- and two-parameter logistic item parameters: An empirical study. *Educational and Psychological Measurement, 46,* 11–21.

Harwell, M. R., & Janosky, J. E. (1991). An empirical study of the effects of small datasets and varying prior variances on item parameter estimation in BILOG. *Applied Psychological Measurement, 15,* 279–291.

Hulin, C. L., Lissak, R. I., & Drasgow, F. (1982). Recovery of two and three parameter logistic item characteristic curves: A Monte Carlo study. *Applied Psychological Measurement, 6,* 249–260.

Levine, M. V., & Rubin, D. F. (1979). Measuring the appropriateness of multiple-choice test scores. *Journal of Educational Statistics, 4,* 269–290.

Lord, F. M. (1968). An analysis of the Verbal Scholastic Aptitude Test using Birnbaum's three-parameter logistic model. *Educational and Psychological Measurement, 28,* 989–1020.

Luecht, R. M. (1998a). CASTISEL (Version 1.5) [Computer software]. Philadelphia: National Board of Medical Examiners.

Luecht, R. M. (1998b). Computer-assisted test assembly using optimization heuristics. *Applied Psychological Measurement, 22,* 224–336.

Luecht, R. M. (2000, April). *Implementing the computer-adaptive sequential testing (CAST) framework to mass produce high quality computer-adaptive and mastery tests.* Paper presented at the annual meeting of the National Council on Measurement in Education, New Orleans, LA.

Luecht, R. M., Brumfield, T., & Breithaupt, K. (2002, April). *A testlet assembly design for the Uniform CPA Examination.* Paper presented at the annual meeting of the National Council on Measurement in Education, New Orleans, LA.

Luecht, R. M., & Nungester, R. J. (1998). Some practical examples of computer-adaptive sequential testing. *Journal of Educational Measurement, 35,* 239–249.

Luecht, R. M., & Nungester, R. J. (2000). Computer-adaptive sequential testing. In W. J. van der Linden & C. A. W. Glas (Eds.), *Computerized adaptive testing: Theory and practice* (pp. 117–128). Dordrecht, The Netherlands: Kluwer Academic.

Meijer, R. R., & Sijtsma, K. (2001). Methodology review: Evaluating person fit. *Applied Psychological Measurement, 25,* 107–135.

Mislevy, R. J., & Bock, R. D. (1990). BILOG 3: Item analysis and test scoring with binary logistic models (Version 3.07) [Computer software]. Mooresville, IN: Scientific Software.

Rost, J. (1990). Rasch model in latent classes: An integration of two approaches to item analysis. *Applied Psychological Measurement, 14,* 271–282.

Stocking, M. L., & Swanson, L. (1993). A method for severely constrained item selection in adaptive testing. *Applied Psychological Measurement, 17,* 277–292.

Swaminathan, H., & Gifford, J. A. (1986). Bayesian estimation in the three-parameter logistic model. *Psychometrika, 51,* 589–601.

van der Linden, W. J. (2000). Constrained adaptive testing with shadow tests. In W. J. van der Linden & C. A. W. Glas (Eds.), *Computerized adaptive testing: Theory and practice* (pp. 27–52). Dordrecht, The Netherlands: Kluwer Academic.

Wood, R. L., & Lord, F. M. (1976). *User's guide to LOGIST* (Research Memorandum 76-4). Princeton, NJ: Educational Testing Service.

Wood, R. L., Wingersky, M. S., & Lord, F. M. (1976). *A computer program for estimating examinee ability and item characteristic curve parameters* (Research Memorandum 76-6). Princeton, NJ: Educational Testing Service.

APPLIED MEASUREMENT IN EDUCATION, *19*(3), 257–260
Copyright © 2006, Lawrence Erlbaum Associates, Inc.

COMMENTARY

Multistage Testing:
Widely or Narrowly Applicable?

Stephen Stark
Department of Psychology
University of South Florida

Oleksandr S. Chernyshenko
Department of Psychology
University of Canterbury, New Zealand

Multistage testing (MST) is a new computerized test delivery technology aimed at enhancing the quality of credentialing exams. MST offers the potential to increase testing efficiency and decision accuracy with respect to traditional linear fixed-length tests (LFTs) or linear parallel forms tests while being more manageable than true item level computerized adaptive tests (CATs). Specifically, MST provides better test security because, with automated test assembly (ATA), it is possible to create many forms that are parallel in content and information, and panels (see Luecht, Brumfield, & Breithaupt, 2006/this issue) can be assigned randomly to examinees within a testing center. Second, MST allows greater control over test construction because subject matter experts have the opportunity to review all panels and conduct analyses examining dimensionality, adverse impact, and differential test functioning prior to publication. Third, because MST administers items in bundles (testlets) rather than individually, problems with sparse operational data matrices for subsequent item recalibration are mitigated. Finally, MST should increase satisfaction among test-takers, with respect to true CATs, because the technology allows examinees to navigate freely within testlets, meaning that items can be skipped and answers can be reviewed or changed before proceeding to the next

Correspondence should be addressed to Stephen Stark, Department of Psychology, University of South Florida, Tampa, FL 33647. E-mail: sstark@cas.usf.edu stage. For these reasons, MST should provide instant appeal to agencies seeking to modernize their examination procedures.

To date, very few published studies have evaluated the virtues and shortcomings of MST. The articles presented in this special issue provide some interesting insights with regard to launching an MST program and the expected gains in reliability and decision accuracy. In the following paragraphs, we briefly review each article and suggest some possible avenues for future research.

In the first article, Leucht et al. (2006/this issue) describe the steps necessary to construct MST panels having a 1-3-3 design via ATA. They present two alternatives for setting the upper and lower bounds on number-correct scores used for routing examinees through each panel. The *approximate maximum information* method uses root-finding techniques to identify theta values where the testlet information functions for adjacent panels (E-M, M-H) intersect. The *defined population intervals* method identifies theta values that could be used to ensure, for example, equal proportions of examinees being routed through a panel's primary pathways. After selecting the theta values by either method, estimated true scores are computed at the respective upper and lower bounds, and examinees are routed by comparing their number-correct score to the boundary score at each stage. It would be interesting to have seen simulation evidence regarding which procedure would be more effective, and by how much, in terms of exposure control and decision accuracy. Future studies should also compare Luecht's (1998) normalized weighted absolute deviation heuristic algorithm for ATA to van der Linden's (1998) linear programming approach, as well as the security and efficiency of different MST designs (as an example, see the 1-3-3, 1-2-2 comparisons in Jodoin, Zenisky, & Hambleton, 2006/this issue).

In the second article, Jodoin et al. (2006/this issue) provide a nice description of how MST lies between LFT and CAT in terms of administrative control and testing efficiency. They emphasize the importance of reliable classification decisions rather than just reliable ability estimates. Their article compares replications of two-stage 40-item MSTs with 60-item three-stage MSTs, a 60-item LFT, and a 60-item "real" test in terms of reliability, scoring, and decision accuracy and consistency. Perhaps surprisingly, there appeared to be no significant differences between true and estimated ability scores across designs; all correlations for the final ability estimates exceeded .9 and differed only in the second or third decimal places. Decision accuracy, false positive, false negative, and kappa values were similar for all 60-item tests regardless of design or passing rate. It is interesting that the two-stage MST did almost as well as the others, despite being one third shorter. This suggests that tests lengths investigated in this article, as well as the other articles, might be too long to reveal any of the psychometric benefits of MST as compared to traditional static tests. In addition, future research might appropriately focus on simulation studies aimed at understanding the source of misclassification decisions. For example, it would be useful to know whether misclassification results primarily from ATA panels failing to achieve target information functions, one or more problematic routes in a panel, or differences between actual and assumed examinee trait distributions.

In the third article, Hambleton and Xing (2006/this issue) compare the effect on decision accuracy of matching the target information function for panels to either the mean of the examinee trait distribution (assumed to be standard normal) or to the passing score (the conventional approach). Unlike in the other articles, these authors used true item-level CAT as a baseline for examining the efficacy of MST. As expected, CAT performed better but, contrary to conventional wisdom, MSTs matched to the mean of the examinee trait distribution yielded somewhat higher classification accuracy than MSTs matched to the passing score. This is a very intriguing finding and should be examined further in subsequent studies, perhaps using trait distributions other than standard normal, as it is quite likely that examinee proficiency in some credential settings might be very skewed.

In the last article, Chuah, Drasgow, and Luecht (2006/this issue) discuss the costs associated with pretesting items for the launch of a MST program. They conducted a simulation study to see how reducing sample size affects the accuracy of classification decisions by way of increased error in estimated item parameters. Similar to other studies, they found that a-parameters tended to be overestimated in samples of 300, leading to overestimation of panel information functions and, thus, an overly optimistic impression of measurement precision. However, ability estimation and classification accuracy were similar for pretest sample sizes of 300 and 1,000, and classification accuracy for the $N = 300$ pretest condition was only 0.5% (!) lower than when the true (generating) item parameters were used for ATA and scoring. This is an extremely important finding because it shows that large pretest samples are not needed for MST administration and ability estimation alone. This should improve test security by reducing the exposure of items before launch. It is important to note that accurate ability estimates and decisions will also be made prior to recalibration with operational data. Of course, as noted by the authors, this assumes that examinees are fully motivated and respond according to the selected IRT model. In practice, test developers must focus on obtaining motivated pretest samples and should consider using procedures to identify aberrant responses (see also Stark, Chernyshenko, & Drasgow, 2005).

In summary, these articles provide a good introduction to MST technology and its possible benefits and limitations. MST clearly offers advantages over CAT in terms of administrative control as well as advantages over LFT with regard to test security. Yet, on the basis of these initial studies, the psychometric improvements of MST over simpler LFT designs remain an open question. Here psychometric gains appeared to be small, but somewhat larger improvements might have been observed if researchers had varied the allocation of items across stages (e.g., longer or shorter initial and final stages), considered different examinee trait distributions, or examined more closely the source of misclassification decisions. In our view, however, the biggest effect on ability estimation and classification accuracy probably lies in test *length* rather than test *design*. In a credentialing context, 40- and 60- item tests might be needed to meet all content specifications, but with tests this long it is unlikely that any adaptive algorithm would provide much improvement over a well-constructed LFT. Nonetheless, in settings where testing time comes at a premium, and where the number of constructs assessed is large (e.g., personnel selection), much shorter tests (15–20 items or fewer) per dimension are required. It is there that MST might provide the expected increases in efficiency over LFT. Otherwise, the cost of MST implementation must be justified primarily by concerns about test security and examinee satisfaction, issues that should be explored in future studies.

REFERENCES

Chuah, S. C., Drasgow, F., & Luecht, R. (2006/this issue). How big is big enough? Sample size requirements for CAST item parameter estimation. *Applied Measurement in Education, 19*, 241–255.

Hambleton, R. K., & Xing, D. (2006/this issue). Optimal and nonoptimal computer-based test designs for making pass–fail decisions. *Applied Measurement in Education, 19*, 221–239.

Jodoin, M. G., Zenisky, A., & Hambleton, R. (2006/this issue). Comparison of the psychometric properties of several computer-based test designs for credentialing exams with multiple purposes. *Applied Measurement in Education, 19*, 203–220.

Luecht, R. M. (1998). Computer-assisted test assembly using optimization heuristics. *Applied Psychological Measurement, 22*, 224–236.

Luecht, R., Brumfield, T., & Breithaupt, K. (2006/this issue). A testlet assembly design for adaptive multistage tests. *Applied Measurement in Education, 19*, 189–202.

Stark, S., Chernyshenko, O. S., & Drasgow, F. (2005). Identifying and understanding the effects of unmotivated examinees on test dimensionality: Application of optimal appropriateness measurement. *International Journal of Testing, 5*, 247–263.

van der Linden, W. J. (1998). Optimal assembly of psychological and educational tests. *Applied Psychological Measurement, 22*, 195–211.

For Product Safety Concerns and Information please contact our EU representative GPSR@taylorandfrancis.com Taylor & Francis Verlag GmbH, Kaufingerstraße 24, 80331 München, Germany

T - #0162 - 270225 - C0 - 229/152/4 - PB - 9780805893717 - Gloss Lamination